TRAVEL + LEISURE'S
unexpected FRANCE

The Place Vendôme, in Paris.
(Overleaf: the village of
Aubrac, in Aveyron.)

TRAVEL + LEISURE'S
unexpected FRANCE

Introduction by Nancy Novogrod
Editor-in-Chief

LONDON, NEW YORK, MUNICH, MELBOURNE, DELHI

For DK

Project Editor	Steve Setford
Art Editor	Peter Radcliffe
Project Manager	Nigel Duffield
Publisher	Sophie Mitchell

For T + L

Editor-in-Chief	Nancy Novogrod
Editor	Alice Gordon
Consulting Editors	Laura Begley, Michael Cain, Nina Willdorf
Photo Editor	Katie Dunn
Project Manager	Meeghan Truelove
Research Editor	Mario Mercado
Project Assistants	Tanvi Chheda, Bree Sposato

First published in the United States in 2007
by DK Publishing, Inc.
375 Hudson Street,
New York, New York 10014

10 9 8 7 6 5 4 3 2

002-FD155-Jan/08

Copyright © 2007, 2011 Dorling Kindersley
Limited
Text copyright © 2007, 2011 Travel + Leisure

A Cataloging-in-Publication record for
this book is available from the Library of
Congress.

ISBN 978-0-7566-2497-2

DK books are available at special discounts
for bulk purchases for sales promotions,
premiums, fund-raising, or educational use.
For details, contact: DK Publishing Special
Markets, 375 Hudson Street, New York, NY
10014 or SpecialSales@dk.com

Color reproduction by GRB, Italy
Printed and bound by Hung Hing, China

Discover more at
www.dk.com

T+L Online:
For more on France, go to
ww.travelandleisure.com

Bread and wine at the vineyards of Domaine Houchart, in Provence.

CONTENTS

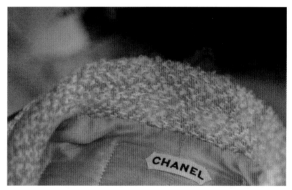

Introduction

FOR MANY PEOPLE, FRANCE IS THE VERY HEART AND SOUL OF EUROPE, FRENCH FOOD IS THE ONLY TRUE CUISINE, AND SPOKEN FRENCH IS THE MOST ELEGANT AND MELODIOUS LANGUAGE IN THE WORLD.

The Champs-Élysées, the Tuileries, the Rive Gauche and Rive Droite are familiar before even setting foot in Paris, and just the name Côte d'Azur conjures up visions of unparalleled glamour and luxury. In fact, getting to know France, and France alone, in all its richness and complexity, can become the life's work of some travelers.

Unexpected France presents a view of the country's pleasures that is at once panoramic and highly selective—pastoral, coastal, urban, encompassing both the old and the new. Carefully compiled by the editors of *Travel + Leisure* from articles published in the magazine, the book includes sections on destinations, places to stay, food and drink, and arts and culture. To make your navigation of the country beyond these pages simpler, a map and resource guide have been included with each story.

Through insider views provided by *Travel + Leisure's* global network of writers and correspondents and with images from the magazine's award-winning photographers, *Unexpected France* uncovers the treasures of each region—the châteaux and gardens of the Loire, the medieval villages clinging to the spectacular cliffs of the Aveyron, a leisurely bike route through Versailles. For hotel enthusiasts, there is that Parisian *ne plus ultra*, the Ritz; new incarnations of Southern French country inns; even gypsy wagons that accept paying guests. For food lovers, we offer *cèpes* and duck confit in the Dordogne, briny oysters in Brittany, the bistros of Provence, and Paris haunts. And, of course, there are shopping options galore.

Intended as both a guide and an inspiration, *Unexpected France* offers you tools for exploration—for the kinds of trips that live on as vibrant memories. And I can assure you, given the many routes outlined here, in *la Belle France* there will always be more great travels ahead.

Nancy Novogrod

The formal 16th-century–style gardens at the Château de Villandry, in the Loire Valley.

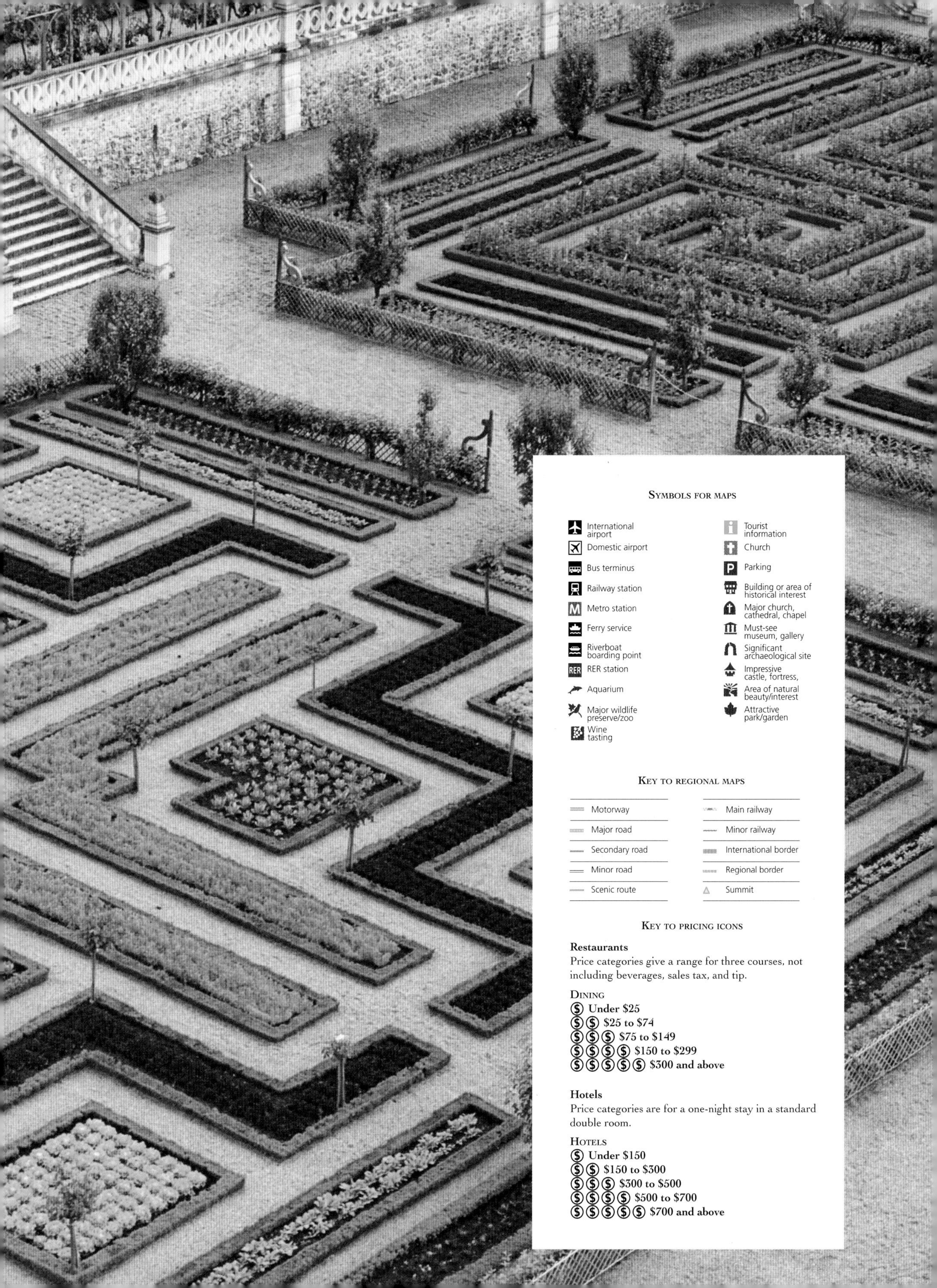

Symbols for Maps

✈	International airport	🛈	Tourist information
✈	Domestic airport	✝	Church
🚌	Bus terminus	🅿	Parking
🚆	Railway station	⛪	Building or area of historical interest
Ⓜ	Metro station	⛪	Major church, cathedral, chapel
⛴	Ferry service	🏛	Must-see museum, gallery
⛴	Riverboat boarding point	⚓	Significant archaeological site
RER	RER station	🏰	Impressive castle, fortress,
🐬	Aquarium	🌲	Area of natural beauty/interest
🦌	Major wildlife preserve/zoo	🍁	Attractive park/garden
🍷	Wine tasting		

Key to Regional Maps

═══	Motorway	····	Main railway
═══	Major road	——	Minor railway
────	Secondary road	▪▪▪	International border
────	Minor road	···	Regional border
────	Scenic route	△	Summit

Key to Pricing Icons

Restaurants
Price categories give a range for three courses, not including beverages, sales tax, and tip.

Dining
$ Under $25
$$ $25 to $74
$$$ $75 to $149
$$$$ $150 to $299
$$$$$ $300 and above

Hotels
Price categories are for a one-night stay in a standard double room.

Hotels
$ Under $150
$$ $150 to $300
$$$ $300 to $500
$$$$ $500 to $700
$$$$$ $700 and above

Catherine de Médicis's Gardens at Château de Chenonceau, in the Loire Valley.

PART ONE
Destinations

Paris Modern

HOW DOES IT FEEL TO RETURN TO A PLACE YOU ONCE CALLED HOME—
AND FIND IT UTTERLY TRANSFORMED? A PARIS DEVOTEE CHARTS THE
CHANGES TO ONE OF THE WORLD'S MOST STYLISH CITIES. BY KATE BETTS

Looking east from the Pont de Tolbiac in the 13th Arrondissement you wouldn't know you were in Paris. As far as the eye can see, there are cranes and glass towers punctuating the rabbit warrens of old working-class neighborhoods. Below, a soundless METEOR train glides by as a girl with an iPod speed-walks past the four glass towers of the Bibliothèque Nationale, toward the Rue Louise Weiss, Paris's thriving arts center. Dressed in gladiator sandals, bug-eyed black sunglasses, and pleated micromini, she looks like a replicant out of *Blade Runner*. This is not the familiar tableau of old Paris, perfectly preserved in snapshots by Robert Doisneau. That view, of the luminous white dome of Sacré Coeur, the iconic Eiffel Tower, and the prickly spire of Notre Dame, is 80 degrees to the west. This is the picture of new Paris.

Everyone who knows Paris has his or her own private set of postcards. Mine is a series of snapshots of the city I saw in my twenties. I lived there for five years and started my professional life as a fashion reporter, chronicling the movements of the couturiers housed along the Faubourg-St.-Honoré. I had a room with a French family in St.-Germain. I got to know a bunch of precocious French girls who came from very good families but spoke like truck drivers and chain-smoked Philip Morris Lights. Domitille, Bibiane, Priscille: each exuded that irresistible nonchalance that is the essence of French style. They were effortlessly brilliant chefs, buying their organic vegetables at the market on the Boulevard Raspail. Every year they fled the city for the month of August, holing up in whitewashed houses on the Île de Ré. They wore creased dark denim jeans from A.P.C. On Saturdays they would throw rumpled trench coats over fishnet stockings and dance the night away at a boîte called Castel's. When they got married and became mothers, they put their babies in tiny Shetland sweaters from a funny little shop on Rue Madame, and stashed away their beat-up Hermès Birkin bags the minute American women began carrying them in a garish shade of orange ostrich, opting, instead, for some soft canvas cargo bag they found at an army-navy store.

A view of Avenue George V and the curvilinear exterior of the restaurant La Suite.

10

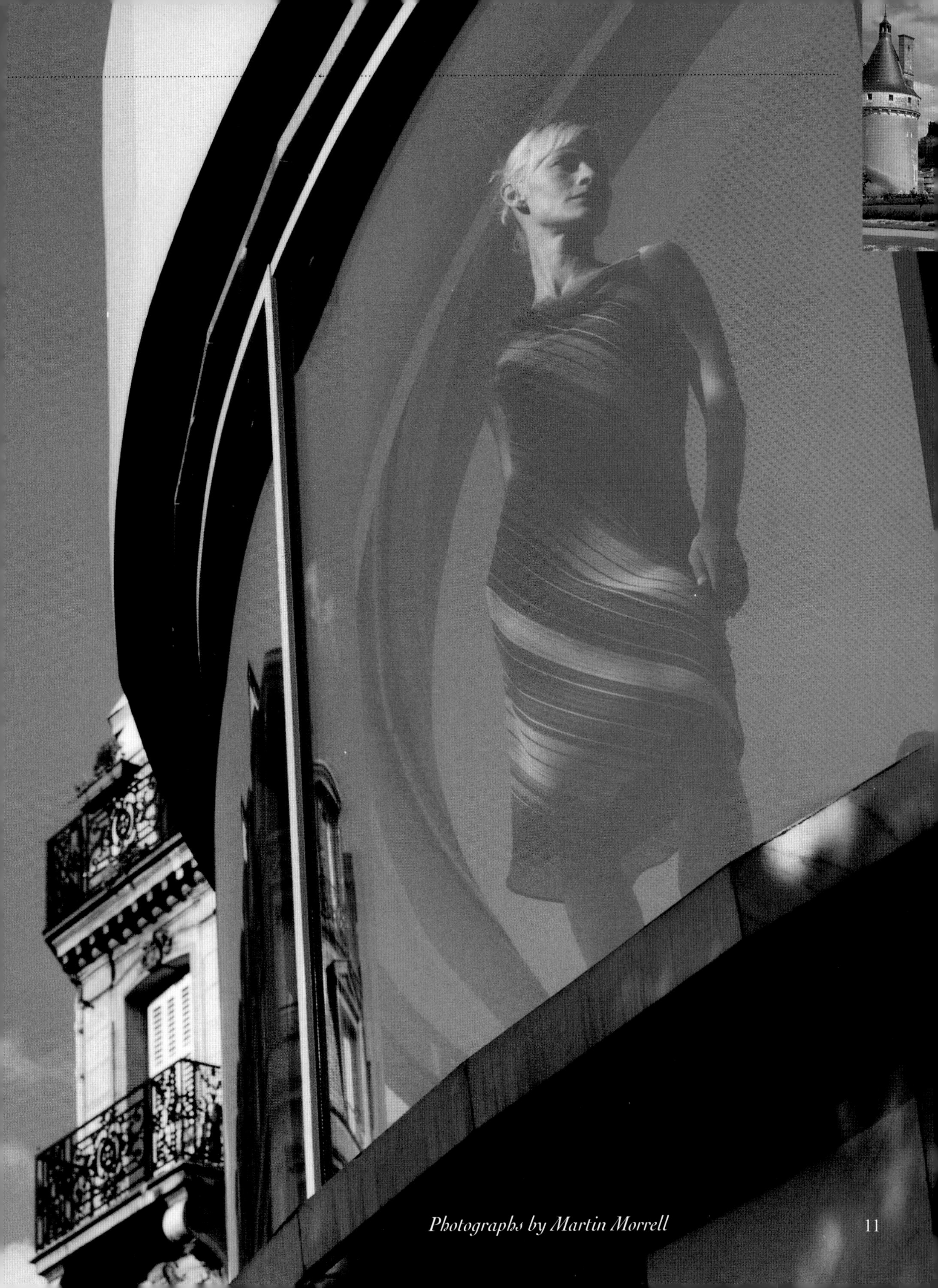

Photographs by Martin Morrell

*Graffiti on
Rue Charlot.*

Later, as a New York–based fashion editor, I made quarterly pilgrimages to the collections every year for a decade, and Paris became my home away from home. As a writer and editor for *Vogue* and then editor in chief of *Harper's Bazaar*, I depended on Paris as a muse, for inspiration. Mine was an almost Pavlovian response: I would catch a whiff of black tobacco and briny Camembert cheese and suddenly I would have ideas for magazine articles. An emerald Christian Lacroix couture dress could inspire a whole page of green products. Two rangy girls sauntering down the Faubourg-St.-Honoré in long bell-bottoms and Françoise Hardy fringes would transform a spring fashion report. But things change—people more than cities, certainly. I dropped out of the fashion business for a bit. Instead of bistro menus and supermodels, I trained my eye on preschool applications and model airplanes. The history I shared with Paris began to fade like an old photograph.

Recently, I found myself returning to Paris again on the bi-annual fashion pilgrimages, this time as the editor of *Time Style & Design*. When I first ventured back, with my husband and son in tow, it had been a few years since I'd seen Paris. Staring out the window, on a bleary, sleep-deprived cab ride in from the airport, I suddenly felt a rush of anticipation and dread as we crossed the Périphérique into central Paris. Would I have the same Pavlovian reaction? Would the prospect of a totally changed city still inspire me? I wanted to discover a Paris I had never seen before and yet I hoped, at the same time, to find everything as I'd left it.

We dumped our bags at Hôtel Le Ste.-Beuve, a charming place we chose for its proximity to the Luxembourg Gardens. My husband and son set off for the puppet shows, excited to discover the Sunday spectacle I'd religiously attended with my goddaughter years before. I ventured south in the direction of the Place St.-Sulpice, to meet my old friend Bibiane. Save for the sleek Yves Saint Laurent boutique not much had changed physically in the neighborhood. The same waiters at the Bar de la Croix Rouge, where I used to steal away from the fashion fray for a Poilâne sandwich, were still rushing around pouring *ballons* of Beaujolais for a crowd that would soon decamp to St.-Tropez and other points south. Students from the Sciences Po still loitered outside Le Basile smoking Gauloises cigarettes. And Bibiane still had her gorgeous 18th-century apartment with double-height ceilings and a

wrought-iron balcony overlooking Rue de Grenelle. On the surface, she had not changed much: she still wore that chic indifference like a favorite old couture jacket and she still knew how to make a delicious meal out of three eggs, some leftover cheese, and a piece of bread. There were subtle differences, though. She'd quit smoking and now had to tolerate the nasty habit in her two eldest kids. She wore sneakers instead of high heels. She talked about America in less reverent tones.

That French-American divide was one I knew too well. During my years in Paris, I'd made every effort to be accepted by the French. I learned the slang, using words like *bringue* and *choper* instead of *fête* or *prendre*. I followed the rigid manners of keeping your hands on the table during meals, and adopted the correct dress code of black tights and high heels. I took weekly invitations to Sunday lunch—the tabernacle of French family life—as signs of success. Yet no matter how I tried, I would always be the American who worked too hard, spoke too loudly, and spent too freely.

So the lingering tension between Americans and the French didn't surprise me on our visit to Paris. For a time after the invasion of Iraq, Americans took to calling the French "Chiraqis." A few days prior to our arrival, our hotel sent a poignant letter of apology by e-mail. "Dear American Friends," it

A view of the glass-and-chrome Bibliothèque Nationale, in the 13th Arrondissement.

read, "the truth is we, the French people, like American folks. Beyond our pride of being French, we greatly admire American people."

In a taxi on my way back to the hotel from Bibiane's place, I encountered my first brush with a different kind of anti-Americanism. "Fashion has not been the same in this city since that guy came around with his 1970's look and his bell-bottom pants," the unusually affable cab driver said when I told him I worked in the fashion business. Which imposter could he mean? Karl Lagerfeld, who had certainly generated years of Gallic vitriol when, as a German, he took over the house of Chanel? Could he mean Alexander McQueen, the trash-talking son of a Cockney taxi driver who was practically chased out of the hidebound house of Givenchy? As we full-throttled it down the ancient cow path known as Rue des Saints-Pères, the subject of the driver's ire came to me: Was it Tom Ford, who took over YSL? "Ah, yes!" he said, punching his fist in the air as if I'd just scored the winning goal of the World Cup finals. Ah, yes! An American had ruined French fashion.

When I told the Israeli-born Lanvin designer Alber Elbaz my story the next day over lunch, he laughed. "Of course, it's Paris, and it took me two

years of living here to accept that," he said. "If it weren't that way, it wouldn't be France and we wouldn't want to be here, would we?" Elbaz described how he had fought French customs at every turn, determined to live as he had in New York — in a loft in a trendy, ungentrified neighborhood, dinners at a different restaurant every night. Eventually he gave up and found himself a bourgeois apartment off the Place des Victoires and ordered steak for lunch every other day at the stuffy bar in the Hôtel de Crillon, around the corner from his office.

Even the best rule-breakers eventually succumb to the Parisian way of life. Over dinner in the upstairs room at Caviar Kaspia, a froufrou favorite of the fashion crowd, Marc Jacobs, the transplanted Louis Vuitton designer who was once a fixture on the New York club scene, cheerily told me how he, too, had embraced bourgeois Paris with gusto. "I never go out at night anymore. I walk Alfred, my dog, on the Champ de Mars, and I go to my neighborhood bakery where everyone knows me," he said. "I like to stay close to home."

My idea of home in Paris is a cracked leather *banquette* in an old family-owned bistro such as Aux Fins Gourmets on Boulevard St.-Germain, where the walls are yellow from so many years of tobacco smoke and where you can still get a simple *salade mixte* and *steak frites* without too much fuss. So I am always amused and intrigued when three-star chefs go into bistro mode. That was the case a few years ago when Alain Ducasse opened his buzzy brasserie, Aux Lyonnais, a former 1890 stockbrokers' haunt he had taken back to its gastronomic roots—complete with old Parisian accoutrements like linen bags stuffed with sourdough bread, and kitchen bowls filled with *cervelle de Canuts*. And, more recently, at the Comptoir du Relais just off the Place de l'Odéon, where Yves Camdeborde of La Régelade fame makes a point of serving classic bistro food in a low-key atmosphere (so low-key there's not much breathing space between tables). Like Camdeborde, Ducasse serves up food so traditional, even the French marvel: *minute steak à la lyonnaise* lands on the table in front of you still sizzling in the frying pan. Every night these places are packed with long-limbed French fashion editors and leathery society types gorging on huge helpings of *bugnes*, Lyon's sweet, chewy answer to the doughnut.

The French are experts when it comes to reverse *snobbisme*. And the best recent incarnation of that old

Room No. 20 at Hôtel Le Ste.-Beuve, near the Luxembourg Gardens.

MAISON
LYONNAISE

RESTAURANT "AUX LYONNAIS

*Aux Lyonnais, in the
Second Arrondissement,
popular with style-
setters after a recent
Alain Ducasse makeover.* 15

Inside the brasserie Aux Lyonnais.

Plate after plate of tiny servings of crab salad and langoustine tempura, along with intense attention from Robuchon's dedicated waiters (many have worked for him for more than two decades), dazzled me.

"The guy is a god," the French garmento on the stool next to me said as he pierced a soufflé of Chartreuse with pistachio ice cream. He had traveled all day from St.-Tropez just to sample Robuchon's food. It had taken him two days to get in, but it was worth it. "I hate the French, they're turncoats," he said. "But when you see a guy like Robuchon, you have to admit that the French have a gift for genius in some areas."

We'd made the rounds of the old haunts—the favorite bistros, the Luxembourg Gardens, the nostalgic walk across the Pont des Arts. So, on a rainy Saturday my husband and I strapped our four-year-old son into a stroller (much to the disapproval of passers-by) and rushed out to explore the Paris we didn't know. We rode the super-sleek, driverless METEOR subway (No. 14) east to the Bibliothèque Nationale, the area Parisian coolhunters call the new Latin Quarter. We crossed the Pont de Tolbiac and poked around Rue Louise Weiss, where gallery owners like Emmanuel Perrotin and Almine Rech attract a fashion-conscious crowd with their monthly openings.

Gallic trick is the "no reservations" policy at sought-after restaurants. Joël Robuchon kicked off the trend when he opened his L'Atelier de Joël Robuchon on the Rue Montalembert. Robuchon, who is considered one of the greats of French cuisine, had disappeared from the scene for a while and returned triumphantly with a completely new concept. From the get-go, Robuchon's "concept" drove Left Bank intellos into a frenzy: no tablecloths, no tables, no reservations (he now does offer them for the first, early seating, at 6:30). His idea was to serve delicious food at a casual bar, like tapas or sushi are. But the no-reservations policy did not sit well with the French *noblesse oblige*.

"I've never seen people get so upset," said Florence Maeght, the owner of Le Rideau de Paris, a shop that sells wonderful reproductions of 18th-century fabrics from Lyons. "He caused a scandal, because nobody could get in. The French were up in arms!"

It took me four tries to secure one of the 37 seats at Robuchon's bar. It was the afternoon of a long weekend when everyone had left town early (including my family), and I sat down to an incredibly precise and delicious *mille-feuille* of vegetables—tomatoes and zucchini with mozzarella—that tasted as though they'd been nestled in a sunny garden in Provence.

Coveted seats at L'Atelier de Joël Robuchon.

At Balenciaga, on Avenue George V, we discovered a similar contemporary artistic spirit. Instead of hiring a traditional architect, the designer Nicolas Ghesquière asked Alsatian artist Dominique Gonzalez Foerster to transform the store into a kind of quasi-subterranean swimming pool—complete with an Yves Klein blue–painted underground passageway to the neighboring accessories boutique. Across town at Surface to Air, pouty punk rockers convened in turquoise miniskirts and matching leg warmers. And traditional perfume shops and pharmacies seemed to pale in comparison with places like Editions de Parfums on the Rue de Grenelle, where fragrances are tested in scent silos built especially so that the customer may experience the perfume as opposed to just spraying it on their wrists.

On my last day in Paris, I stopped by Loulou de la Falaise's shop in the heart of the First Arrondissement. Here was a fashion muse if ever there was one, inspiring Saint Laurent for more than 30 years and creating his iconic accessories. The kaleidoscope colors on the walls and the display cases filled with exotic beaded necklaces reminded me of the days when I used to sneak backstage at Saint Laurent's shows. Crouching in a corner, the photographer Roxanne Lowit and I would watch Loulou's every move and, mostly, what she wore— animal print silk blouses, Russian Cossack jackets, brightly colored peasant skirts. Something about her style—their style—seemed so effortless and yet so achievable. They represented old Paris, the part of the city that doesn't change even as the world around it does. Yet despite their bourgeois rigidity, the French have an uncanny ability to move with the times. And when Tom Ford took over the house of Saint Laurent, Loulou set about her own course of reinvention, creating a line of chic handbags, tartan quilts, and dramatic costume jewelry—all of it as successful as her style has always been.

I walked back to the hotel via my favorite route: up Rue Madame. The long afternoon light was casting a shadow across the street. Another generation of noisy kids with bulky satchels and freshly scrubbed faces pressed past me on their way to the gardens, just as they had 17 years before. Along the way I clocked my former shopping haunts. Jamin Puech was still selling its hippie macramé handbags, this time sprinkled with old coins. In the window at Le Pont Traversé there was a first edition

Oscar Wilde for sale. Oona L'Ourse, the store where my Parisian pals used to buy those tiny Shetland sweaters for their babies, was still there, too. I ducked in to see if there was anything new— perhaps something for my son. It was a comforting place, but it felt claustrophobic. I didn't even bother to buy one of the adorable sweaters.

Back at the hotel I called Bibiane to say good-bye. She sounded agitated and distracted. She had just learned that she and her family were being evicted from their apartment on Rue de Grenelle, where they had lived for 20 years. I felt a pang of sadness; it was my first apartment in Paris, too. But Bibiane put a brave face on it.

"At first I was so pissed off," she said in her best truck driver slang. "I thought, *Merde*. Now I've come to accept it; in fact, I look at it as a good thing. Change is good."

At that moment, in that city, it seemed she was right.

Tartan-lined fur at Loulou de la Falaise's boutique in the First Arrondissement.

17

Travelers' Guide to Paris

GETTING THERE

From the United States there are regular flights to Paris on American, United, Northwest, Continental, Delta, British Airways, and more. From Canada, Air France and Air Canada fly direct to Paris.

0 meters 500
0 yards 500

For map key see p.7

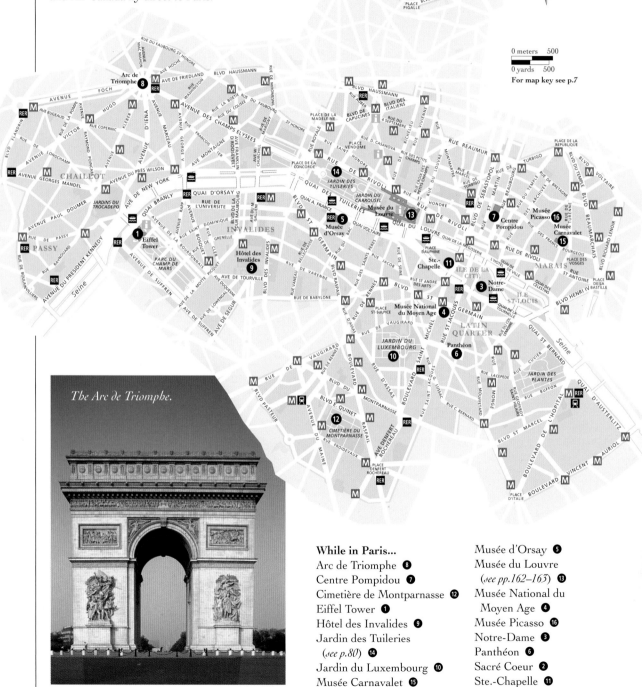

The Arc de Triomphe.

While in Paris...

Arc de Triomphe ❽
Centre Pompidou ❼
Cimetière de Montparnasse ❷
Eiffel Tower ❶
Hôtel des Invalides ❾
Jardin des Tuileries
  (*see p.80*) ⓮
Jardin du Luxembourg ❿
Musée Carnavalet ⓯

Musée d'Orsay ❺
Musée du Louvre
  (*see pp.162–163*) ⓭
Musée National du
  Moyen Age ❹
Musée Picasso ⓰
Notre-Dame ❸
Panthéon ❻
Sacré Coeur ❷
Ste.-Chapelle ⓫

TOP SIGHTS IN PARIS

Arc de Triomphe ❽
Napoleon's triumphal arch, celebrating his victories, was completed in 1836. Standing proudly at the top of the Champs-Elysées, it is now a focal point for rallies, parades, and public events.

Centre Pompidou ❼
Looking like a building turned inside out, the Pompidou (designed by Richard Rogers, Renzo Piano, and Gianfranco Franchini) is home to the Musée Nationale d'Art Moderne. Among the schools represented are Fauvism, Cubism, and Surrealism.

Eiffel Tower ❶
Gustave Eiffel's 1,063-foot tower was maligned by critics when it was built for the 1889 Universal Exhibition, but its graceful symmetry soon made it a star attraction. Ascend to the top for spectacular views.

Hôtel des Invalides ❾
The imposing structure was built from 1671 to 1676 by Louis XIV for wounded and homeless veterans. At its center lies the Sun King's golden-roofed Dôme church, the last resting place of Napoleon Bonaparte.

Jardin du Luxembourg ❿
A green oasis covering 60 acres in the heart of the Left Bank, this is the most popular park in Paris. The gardens, with their broad avenues and formal terraces, are centered around the Palais du Luxembourg.

Musée d'Orsay ❺
This former railway station is now one of the world's leading art galleries. The wonderful collection covers a variety of art forms from the 1848–1914 period, including a notable Impressionist section.

Musée National du Moyen Age ❹
Set in recreated medieval gardens, this museum is a unique combination of Gallo-Roman ruins incorporated into a 15th-century mansion. It houses a superb collection of medieval art.

Notre-Dame ❸
This great Gothic cathedral, founded on the site of a Roman temple, was completed in 1334. A repository of French art and history, it also represents both the spiritual and geographical heart of the country.

Panthéon ❻
The Panthéon was built as a church between 1764 and 1790. Soon after its completion, with the Revolution underway, it was turned into a memorial to the good and the great of France. It now houses the remains of Voltaire, Victor Hugo, and many other illustrious French citizens.

Sacré Coeur ❷
This white-domed basilica was built as a memorial to the French soldiers killed in the Franco-Prussian War (1870–71). The terrace affords one of the best free views over Paris.

Sainte-Chapelle ❿
Called a "gateway to Heaven," this magical medieval chapel was built in 1248 by Louis IX to house Christ's purported Crown of Thorns (now in the treasury of Notre-Dame).

St.-Sulpice dominates the rooftops of the Sixth Arrondissement.

PARIS ARRONDISSEMENTS
The districts, or *arrondissements*, of Paris are numbered from 1 to 20. The first three numbers of the postcode – 750 (sometimes 751) – indicate Paris; the last two give the *arrondissement* number. The postcode of the First Arrondissement is *75001*.

WHERE TO STAY

The Left Bank properties that the French like to call *hôtels de charme* are always appealing, for their proximity to the Jardin du Luxembourg and surrounding cafés. Sometimes "charm" translates into minuscule, so make sure you ask for a deluxe room.

Hôtel Le Ste.-Beuve
Interiors are crisp and comfortable, courtesy of David Hicks, but the real attraction is the central location. Ask for room No. 22 on the top floor.
9 Rue Ste.-Beuve, Sixth Arr.;
33-1/45-48-20-07;
hotel-sainte-beuve.fr;
doubles from $$.

Hôtel Montalembert
They call it the Ritz of the Left Bank, and with reason: rooms are pricey (though bigger than most), service is very good, and every room has wireless Internet access. The restaurant is the top lunch place for Paris's book-publishing world. In warm weather, opt for drinks or dinner on the terrace.
3 Rue de Montalembert, Seventh Arr.;
33-1/45-49-68-68;
montalembert.com;
doubles from $$$$.

Pot de la cuisinière,
at Aux Lyonnais.

The Palais du Luxembourg, viewed from the classically designed gardens.

Hôtel Pont Royal
This hotel, which is big for the Left Bank (10 suites in addition to 65 rooms), has a gorgeous panoramic view of Paris from the penthouse suite. But the real secret of the place is the room service provided by Joël Robuchon's L'Atelier, which is located downstairs.
7 Rue de Montalembert, Seventh Arr.;
33-1/45-49-68-68;
doubles from $$$$.

Hôtel Verneuil
Though the hotel is tiny, you would be hard-pressed to find a better deal in the middle of Paris. There's minimal computer access and few modern amenities, but the service is great: Joseph the night watchman will serve you coffee and juice on the morning of an early departure.
8 Rue de Verneuil,
Seventh Arr.;
33-1/42-60-82-14;
hotelverneuil.com;
doubles from $$.

WHERE TO EAT

Aux Fins Gourmet
Bistro classics like steak frites *and cassoulet.*
213 Blvd. St.-Germain, Seventh Arr.;
33-1/42-22-06-57;
dinner for two $$$.

Aux Lyonnais
32 Rue St.-Marc, Second Arr.;
33-1/42-96-65-04;
dinner for two $$.

Bar de la Croix Rouge
For open-faced sandwiches on toasted Poilâne bread.
Place de la Croix Rouge, Sixth Arr.;
33-1/45-448-06-45;
lunch for two $$.

Casa Bini
The superb food at this neighborhood Italian spot is a good option when you've had enough of heavy French dishes.
36 Rue Gregoire de Tours, Sixth Arr.;
33-1/46-34-05-60;
dinner for two $$$.

Chez Georges
A typical bourgeois bistro known for its sole meunière—and the warm greeting from the family who have owned it forever.
1 Rue du Mail, Second Arr.;
33-1/42-60-07-11;
dinner for two $$$.

L'Atelier de Joël Robuchon
This famed spot has begun to offer reservations for the first seating, at 6:30. Otherwise, try your luck at the door.
5 Rue de Montalembert, Seventh Arr.;
33-1/42-22-56-56;
lunch or dinner for two $$$$.

Ladurée
Service is often sketchy, but it's worth the wait for the famous macaroons, in 15 flavors.
21 Rue Bonaparte, Sixth Arr.
33-1/44-07-64-87;
dinner for two $$$.

Lavinia
A sleek shop that carries thousands of wines, including bottles dating back to 1900. The restaurant serves salads and wines by the glass.
5 Blvd. de la Madeleine, First Arr.;
33-1/42-97-20-27;
lunch for two $$$.

Le Comptoir du Relais
Classic bistro food by chef Yves Camdeborde. No reservations on weekends or for lunch.
9 Carrefour de L'Odeon;
33-1/43-29-12-05;
lunch for two $$$.

WHERE TO SHOP

Au Nom de La Rose
A tiny shop filled with fresh roses. They also sell travel candles.
46 Rue du Bac; Seventh Arr.;
33-1/42-22-22-12.

Autour de Christophe Robin
Models swear by the hair-care products from one of the world's great colorists.
9 Rue Guénégaud, Sixth Arr.;
33-1/42-60-99-15;
colorist.net.

Bon Marché
The department store gives shoppers an overview of what's in fashion. The food hall is great for a snack, and the basement has a good selection of wooden toys and crafts.
24 Rue de Sèvres, Seventh Arr.

Bonton
Bonpoint's creators have given birth to this loftlike emporium specializing in cotton separates for newborns to 10-year-olds, and to the cute kids' barbershop next door.
82 Rue de Grenelle, Seventh Arr.;
33-1/44-39-09-20.

Du Pareil au Même
For inexpensive preppy Parisian kids' clothes and shoes.
14 Rue St.-Placide, Sixth Arr.;
33-1/45-44-04-40;
dpam.com.

Éditions de Parfums Frédéric Malle
This is the place for unique fragrances by the masters of the trade.
21 Rue Mont Thabor, First Arr.;
33-1/42-22-77-22;
editionsdeparfums.com.

Hervé Chapelier
Brightly colored nylon bags of all sizes in which to carry everything home.
1 bis Rue du Vieux-Colombier, Sixth Arr.;
33-1/44-07-06-50.

Huilerie Artisanale J. Leblanc et Fils
A petite shop stocked with delicious hand-pressed oils made from olives, pignoli, and pistachios.
6 Rue Jacob, Sixth Arr.;
33-1/46-34-61-55;
huile-leblanc.com.

Iris
Designer shoes by the likes of Marc Jacobs, Paul Smith, and Proenza-Schouler.
28 Rue de Grenelle, Seventh Arr.;
33-1/42-22-89-81.

Jamin Puech
One-of-a-kind handbags at the French designer's original shop.
43 Rue Madame, Sixth Arr.;
33-1/45-48-14-85;
jamin-puech.com.

Le Pont Traversé
Rare and used books.
62 Rue de Vaugirard, Sixth Arr.;
33-1/45-48-06-48.

Le Rideau de Paris
Florence Maeght (of Fondation Maeght in the south of France) sells quilts and curtains in reproduction 18th-century prints from Lyons. Custom-order anything.
32 Rue du Bac, Seventh Arr.;
33-1/42-61-18-56;
le-boutis.com.

Maria Luisa
Fashion stylists flock to Maria Luisa Poumaillou's shop for guidance and sharp pieces by Jean Paul Gaultier, Ann Demeulemeester, Givenchy, and others.
2 Rue Cambon, First Arr.;
33-1/47-03-96-15.

Oona L'Ourse
Where the children in the Luxembourg Gardens get their Shetland sweaters and English Start Rite shoes.
72 Rue Madame, Sixth Arr.;
33-1/42-84-11-94;
oonalourse.com.

Simrane
Indian cotton printed napkins, tablecloths, and accessories.
23 or 25 Rue Bonaparte, Sixth Arr.;
33-1/43-54-90-73 or 33-1/46-33-98-71.

SEE ALSO
For more on Paris:
Puttin' on the Ritz pp.80–81
Living Rooms pp.162–163
Coco Loco pp.190–191

The Eiffel Tower, in the Seventh Arrondissement.

Biking Through Versailles

BEYOND THE FORMAL GARDENS AND FOUNTAINS OF LOUIS XIV'S PALACE THERE IS THE POWERFUL ENCHANTMENT OF PRISTINE COUNTRYSIDE. BY JOAN JULIET BUCK

VERSAILLES

The past is another country, and it's the only place I ever want to go. When the air collects into soup at the bottom of the bowl that Paris sits in, and the lady in the market corrects my request for "two pieces of roast beef" to "two slices" with a withering look, and I become too weary to rise above the passive-aggressive subtext in every exchange, I flee to a place of total and utter bliss. It's 20 minutes away by cab and three-and-a-half centuries away in the past. When I edited *Paris Vogue*, my greatest and sometimes only pleasure consisted in bicycling through the vast park of Versailles. In the autumn, the overgrown *allées* of

The cross-shaped Grand Canal stretches beyond André Le Nôtre's formal gardens at Versailles.

Photographs by Benoît Peverelli

the former hunting grounds were bumpy with fallen horse chestnuts; in the winter, I raced around the endless perimeter of the Grand Canal to keep warm; and on summer evenings, I rocked my melancholy by the empty basins of stone fountains.

Grandiose and overwhelming, Versailles stands for everything pompous about France. In 1661, Louis XIV took over a marsh west of Paris to build the best palace in the world. He added the Trianon as a pocket palace where he could hang out and be a family man. Louis XV built the Petit Trianon for Madame de Pompadour, and Louis XVI created Le Hameau, a little farm of half-timbered cottages, for Marie-Antoinette. The Revolution trashed them all, and then for two centuries, punctilious curators reassembled the treasures while savant gardeners snipped and seeded the grounds. In 2006, Versailles became fashionable again, because of Sofia Coppola's movie, *Marie Antoinette*, which was filmed in its great rooms for the comparatively reasonable cost of $20,000 a day. The hordes of tourists trundling along the Hall of Mirrors will now ask where Kirsten Dunst sat to look at the roll of silk and exclaim, unforgettably, "Wow!"

The formal gardens and vistas of Le Nôtre are well-known and punishing to the feet, but Versailles has the unknown bounty of a magical, carefully tended 17th-century park, whose dimensions and details exceed the reach of any map or any

The author biking past
Versailles's Grand Canal.

Le Nôtre's Parterre du Midi, the south flowerbed.

Marie-Antoinette's sheep graze just beyond a light wire fence. Despite Elizabeth's urging, Pearl does not recognize the sheep as sheep; summer-shorn and naked, they look faintly human. The Hameau is ahead of us, its Temple de l'Amour visible beyond the trees, but I make a sharp left at the end of the allée, into the avenue that goes past both Trianons. Trees planted in straight lines lead the eye to the Grand Canal. I pause to see the look on Elizabeth's face. Her eyes are wider than ever. "Just wait!!" I shout and speed off, down to the edge of the Grand Canal, where I veer right, as always. Here the trees race staccato on the left, the water is bounded by a white stone ledge just beyond the trees, and the woods on the right are dense with grass.

The first right turn on the cross-shaped canal leads to the side of the Grand Trianon. My parents and grandparents were mad enough, when I was a child, to rent a pink marble house in Le Vésinet, named Le Palais Rose and modeled after the Trianon, so that the real Trianon is an overscaled reminder of an overscaled childhood. But the temptation to do a grandiose memory lane number doesn't slow me down; we have to get to the fields. I ride past the Trianon's Fer à Cheval fountain and into the strange Allée de Bally, where the straight line of trees is suddenly brushed with long grasses, the shade is thicker, and strollers and other bikers immediately vanish, as if no one wanted to go that way. True, there is a round red-and-white *sens interdit* sign on a bollard at the entrance to the *allée*, but I do not go to Versailles to obey signs.

At the end of the Allée de Bally is virgin

guidebook. You can ride for hours without seeing a trace of today. It was meant to be experienced on horseback, and a bicycle is lower than a horse, but it never shies, bucks, or needs water, and when you look up as you pedal along, the carefully trimmed trees unfold in perfect symmetry above your head, and the subtle Pythagorean perfections of French ideals realign you into harmony.

One summer, I was working on a play in Paris for two months with Actors Studio director Elizabeth Kemp, living in a hovel, hauling bags full of shoes and props up and down the steep staircases of Montmartre. Elizabeth's dog, an elegant gray border collie named Pearl, desperately needed to herd some sheep. I rarely take anyone to my Versailles, but Elizabeth and Pearl were as town-worn as I was. On our first day off, we found a cabdriver who did not howl at the prospect of conveying a border collie to Versailles, and two tunnels, a bridge, and 25 minutes later we drew up to the gate called the Grille de la Reine, where you can rent large, sturdy bicycles.

In the park after several years away, I feel like a child released from boarding school. I check the wheels on our bikes before I give the Peruvian gentleman who runs the stand my driver's license so he knows we won't vanish. Pearl trots along next to Elizabeth while I set off to the right, down the long road where my legs and arms rediscover the effortless rhythms of the journey. Descendants of

The author with Elizabeth Kemp and Pearl on the Allée de Bally.

Versailles has the unknown bounty of a magical, carefully tended 17th-century park, whose dimensions and details exceed the reach of any map or any guidebook

countryside: fields of wildflowers as far as the eye can see. Pearl dives into the flowers and jumps through the high grass like a flying fish, appearing and vanishing in a feathery arc of gray fur. The dog has caught my bliss.

We head down through a field that ends in 17th-century farm buildings. Just beyond a tall wall is the Ferme de Gally, where children can pet goats and learn all about aubergines, and one summer I spent so long in a high corn maze that at 6 p.m., I found the door in the wall locked and was condemned to pedal along the side of a highway on the Peruvian's worst bike.

Incongruous little biplanes from the 1920's sputter through the sky, rising from a nameless airfield. As we ride across the far edge of the Grand Canal, the long palace of Versailles shimmering large in the distance, we come across two beautiful houses and another farm.

"I want a billionaire so I can have all this!" Elizabeth shouts from her bike.

"I am grateful to the Revolution because all this is already mine!!" I shout back.

Pedaling furiously along the last, southern edge of the Grand Canal, we arrive at the gates that separate Le Nôtre's gardens from the larger park, ride through them and around the Bassin d'Apollon, and come to rest at the shack where I always buy my third bottle of mineral water. "Gift shop?" asks Elizabeth hopefully. Miniature reproductions of Versailles clocks and tiny ornate slippers rendered in painted resin have indeed joined the postcards and the ice cream. A last desperate effort of thigh muscles returns us to the Peruvian, who hands back my driver's license and takes $64.50 for four hours for two. Pearl drags her tail behind us to the Trianon Palace hotel, which sits just outside the Grille de la Reine. We stagger into the bar, fall onto a sofa, and order an Eloise feast of smoked salmon and rare beef with horseradish and, *s'il vous plaît, de l'eau pour le chien.*

Bicycles lined up for rent at the Grille de la Reine.

One of the entrances to Versailles.

Travelers' Guide to Versailles

WHEN TO GO
The park is glorious just about any time of the year. On weekdays it is practically empty.

GETTING THERE
From Paris, take the RER train (to the Versailles Rive Gauche station) or a taxi, which costs $60–$85. Be warned: it is not always easy to get a cab back to Paris.

The Colonnade.

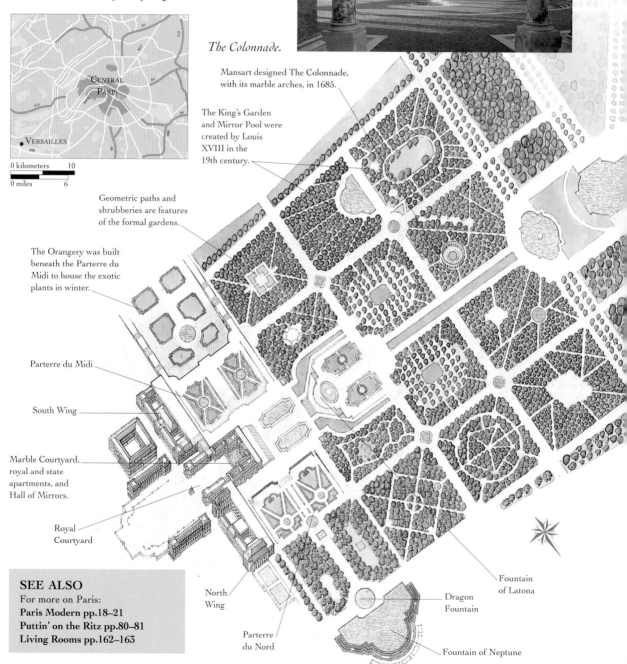

CENTRAL PARIS

• VERSAILLES

0 kilometers 10

0 miles 6

Mansart designed The Colonnade, with its marble arches, in 1685.

The King's Garden and Mirror Pool were created by Louis XVIII in the 19th century.

Geometric paths and shrubberies are features of the formal gardens.

The Orangery was built beneath the Parterre du Midi to house the exotic plants in winter.

Parterre du Midi

South Wing

Marble Courtyard, royal and state apartments, and Hall of Mirrors.

Royal Courtyard

North Wing

Parterre du Nord

Fountain of Latona

Dragon Fountain

Fountain of Neptune

SEE ALSO
For more on Paris:
Paris Modern pp.18–21
Puttin' on the Ritz pp.80–81
Living Rooms pp.162–163

EXPLORING VERSAILLES

The present palace, started by Louis XIV in 1668, grew around Louis XIII's original hunting lodge. Architect Louis Le Vau built the first section, which expanded into an enlarged courtyard. From 1678, Jules Hardouin-Mansart added north and south wings and the Hall of Mirrors. He also designed the chapel, completed in 1710. The opera house (L'Opéra) was added by Louis XV in 1770. André Le Nôtre enlarged the gardens and broke the monotony of the symmetrical layout with expanses of water and creative use of uneven ground.

Great state occasions were held in the Hall of Mirrors, along the west façade, where 17 huge mirrors face tall arched windows.

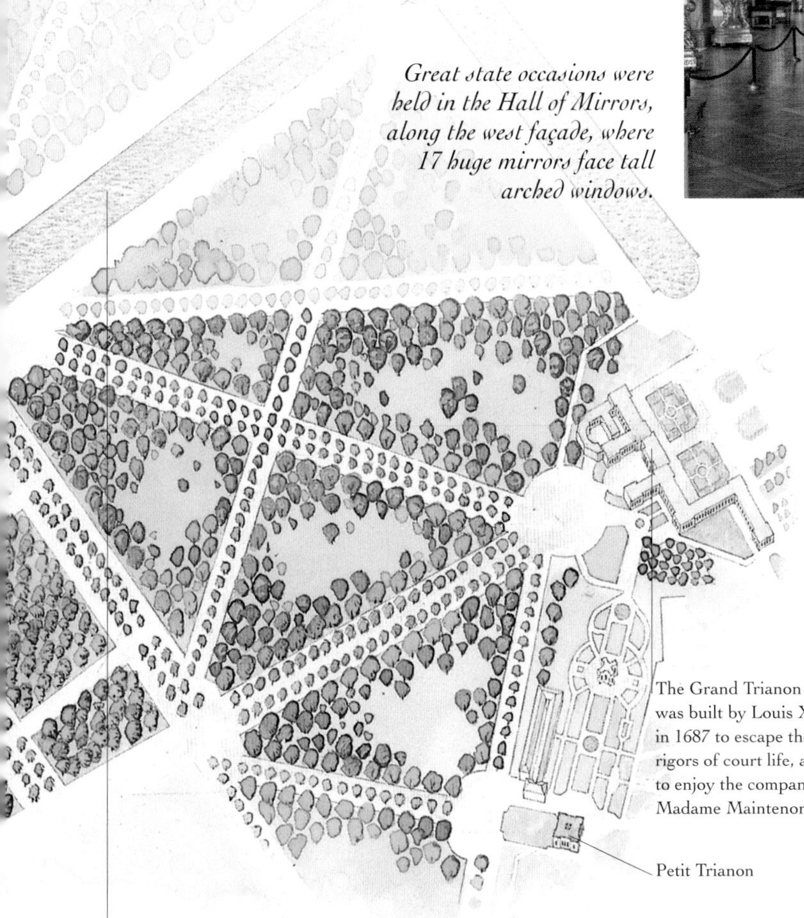

The Grand Trianon was built by Louis XIV in 1687 to escape the rigors of court life, and to enjoy the company of Madame Maintenon.

Petit Trianon

The Grand Canal was the setting for Louis XIV's boating parties.

Built in 1762 as a retreat for Louis XV, the Petit Trianon was a favorite of Marie-Antoinette.

WHERE TO STAY

Trianon Palace & Spa
Choose a room overlooking the palace if you want secondhand son et lumière. *There's a pool and a lavish spa in the basement.*
1 Blvd. de la Reine;
33-1/30-84-50-00;
starwood.com;
doubles $$$.

WHERE TO EAT

La Brasserie du Théâtre
An authentic brasserie.
15 Rue des Réservoirs;
33-1/39-50-03-21;
lunch for two $$.

La Flottille
A restaurant-café on the Grand Canal.
33-1/39-51-41-58;
lunch for two $$.

Les Trois Marches
The Trianon hotel's restaurant offers a "Marie-Antoinette" menu Tuesdays through Fridays.
1 Blvd. de la Reine;
33-1/39-50-13-21;
lunch for two $$$$$.

WHERE TO RENT BIKES

Astel *(33-1/39-66-97-66)* runs three rental stands in the park. Our favorite is at Grille de la Reine.

Introducing Aveyron

THIS SPARSELY POPULATED, OFTEN-OVERLOOKED *DÉPARTEMENT* IN SOUTHERN FRANCE EMBRACES A GORGEOUS, VARIED LANDSCAPE, MEDIEVAL VILLAGES, AND INCOMPARABLE FOOD AND LODGING. BY MARCELLE CLEMENTS

AVEYRON

Clearly, it is always a mistake to arrive in a French provincial capital on a Sunday, unless you are looking to understand why Madame Bovary felt she had to have some action or die. There is no slower clock in all of space and time than that which ticks and tocks in the south of France on the day of rest, and no bell tolls with less urgency than that of the cathedral in Rodez. Mind you, this bell tower, rising up nearly 300 feet and surmounted by a Virgin, is a sumptuous gem of late Gothic Flamboyant style, surging out of a colossal red sandstone edifice begun in the 13th century and finished in the 16th. Three hundred years! Why the hurry? But then, that's one of the attractions of medieval architecture, created by people who didn't even have a word for the future or a concept of progress. The only escape from the present was eternity.

The village of Aubrac, in Aveyron.

Photographs by Christopher Baker

In the shadow of the Rodez cathedral, the Place d'Armes is deserted. I am the sole customer in the one open café. Luckily, I order a traditional Aveyron dish called *aligot*, for which an astonishingly elastic local cheese is slowly stirred into garlicky mashed potatoes, producing a dense, instantly addictive purée. It's comforting enough to push aside thoughts of eternity and even my anxiety about the immediate future: figuring out a trajectory for the next few weeks with only a guidebook that fails to tell me much of anything about most of the points on the map, not to mention the wide spaces between.

It's very quiet here.

Aveyron, with Rodez at its center, is perhaps the least-known *département* in France, one of the biggest and most sparsely populated. "Even in the summer," local people say, "there are still more cows here than tourists." Few Americans have heard of it unless they remember that François Truffaut's film *The Wild Child* was based on the true story of Victor of Aveyron, a young boy who was found in 1798 in the forest, hirsute, naked, and mute. I myself knew next to nothing about it, although I often travel in France, where I was born. This is *la France profonde*, the heartland, which Parisians seldom visit and cannot fathom, where there is some of the world's most stunning, geologically diverse countryside—much of it unspoiled. Aveyron is in the rugged Midi-Pyrénées region in the south, and part of the Massif Central, a huge elevation formed by fire and ice. Peaceful lakeside resorts are an hour's drive from vertiginous peaks, waterfalls, and mind-blowing chasms, under which flow subterranean rivers. Deep valleys alternate with eerie and vast limestone plateaus, or segue into undulating meadows, peat bogs, and hot springs. Some of Aveyron's caves are big enough to shelter the Rodez cathedral.

Here are a thousand castles, more than a thousand megalithic tombs, innumerable Gallo-Roman ruins, and some of the most remarkable Romanesque architecture in Europe, as well as Norman Foster's architectural marvel, the Millau Viaduct—the world's tallest bridge and an unmatched feat of engineering and green planning. Aveyron has five bastides—planned walled towns that were the first urban experiments, built in the 13th century—and 304 communes (more or less equivalent to counties), some a mere handful of houses hanging on to a cliff, others nestled among the caves where prehistoric people lived, still others clustered near thermal baths or scattered downhill from a 12th-century fortress. Ten villages in Aveyron (the highest concentration in any department) meet the 30-odd criteria required to be officially included among the "Most Beautiful Villages of France."

Market day in the town of Rodez.

After lunch, I walk along the silent old streets to the Musée Fenaille—one of the few other places open on Sunday. The collection is astounding, starting with fossils more than 300,000 years old, continuing through the Gallo-Roman heyday, then into the tumultuous Middle Ages, when Aveyron (then called Rouergue) was successively invaded by Visigoths, the counts of Toulouse, and, of course, the English, during the Hundred Years' War. My favorite objects are the statue-menhirs, anthropomorphic standing stones several feet high, carved 4,000 to 5,000 years ago. The Lady of St. Sernin, the most famous piece here, is so well preserved you can see every marking—the hands, the feet, the strange tattoos or scars on her cheeks, the dots for eyes and small circles for breasts, though she has no mouth. What might she say, if she had one? "Hello to you, from 50 centuries ago..."? Or maybe just, "I'm thirsty."

I intend only to glance at the other exhibits on my way out but wind up staying until the museum closes, inspecting objects used by the Ruteni tribe when the city was a hub of southern Gaul (*ruteni* from the Latin for red, the color they dyed their hair). They were fearsome archers and some 12,000 of them fought alongside Vercingetorix, leader of the Gauls, in a heroic revolt against the Romans. But they could also read and write, and the extraordinary exhibit that re-creates one of their pottery shops includes remnants of their bookkeeping. Bookkeepers in Gaul! With dyed red hair! When I come out of the museum, it's easy to see Rodez as a 2,000-year-old city, Gallo-Roman ruins as more immersion course than tourist attraction, and Aveyron as a place with a rare relationship to time—an intimate, uninterrupted connection to the past.

In my rented Renault the following afternoon, I feel slightly guilty hurtling past a couple of Most Beautiful Villages but am determined to reach Laguiole, the main town in the Aubrac region of Aveyron—and the closest one to Michel Bras's restaurant and hotel—before dark. As the road ascends, the temperature drops, and the vegetation changes. Here in mountainous northern Aveyron, the architecture is plainer, the aesthetic more austere. Still, having glimpsed some of the gorgeous towns nearby, I am surprised by Laguiole's modesty.

Statue-menhirs (4,000- to 5,000-year-old monoliths depicting humans) at Rodez's Musée Fenaille.

Aveyron native *Michel Bras, master of*
cuisine du terroir, *in his herb garden*
near Laguiole, in the Aubrac region.

Aubrac's cattle are famed for their meat throughout France.

The municipal parking lot is dominated by the statue of an egregiously stocky bull—no doubt in honor of Aubrac cattle, famous throughout France for their hardy spirit and delicious meat. Farther along, cars obscure the grimy main strip. Clearly, twee is not what visitors to Laguiole are seeking.

I'm growing increasingly fond of speaking with people in the storefront *offices de tourisme* in Aveyron's villages. These are found all over France, but the staffs' encyclopedic knowledge of their domain seems especially indispensable in heritage-rich Aveyron. According to Bruno da Silva in the Laguiole office, connoisseurs come here year after year—many of them choosing to avoid summer and arrive in May and June, or September and October. "Often what these visitors want is *se ressourcer*," he says, using an untranslatable French locution referring to a vacation that returns one to something authentic and pure and restores one's physical and spiritual strength—overlapping perfectly, therefore, with what is known here as *le tourisme vert*, or green tourism.

The other word one hears constantly in Aveyron is *terroir*—meaning both soil and region. Michel Bras is a master of *cuisine du terroir* and Aveyron's most famous native son, and his Michelin three-starred restaurant is reputed to be one of the best in France. Ten minutes up the road from Laguiole, at the end of a longish driveway, there it is, a futuristic metal-and-glass structure lightly poised on an immense carpet of vegetation, which in the waning light seems bright with flowers. Just beyond, a few low-lying

structures constitute the hotel, recalling the shape of the traditional long, squat, gray Aveyron farmhouse, the *buron*, one of Europe's earliest forms of architecture. Down a flight of stone steps, my room is large, luminous, and sober. Two of the walls are mostly glass, and there is hardly any sense of separation from the sumptuous, slightly undulating green expanse outside. Mesmerized by dusk's invasion, I don't draw the curtains until the sky is dark and a faraway sprinkling of lights materializes in Laguiole. My bed is huge and the sheets are indescribably fine. There's no time to memorize the particulars of an almost wild sense of well-being before I fall asleep.

The next morning, I am permitted to visit the kitchen, in which more than 20 people chop, mix, and stir at the customary stations, and at one more station, dedicated to vegetables, two young men peel and trim abundant brightly hued roots, leaves, and flowers. "They are preparing the *gargouillou*, a dish containing more than fifty vegetables," Véronique Bras, Michel Bras's daughter-in-law, tells me. Véronique's husband, Sébastien, works alongside his father in the kitchen, and their children and Michel Bras's parents are close at hand. Four generations of the family live here in the Aubrac region. Each one greets visitors with a quiet cordiality highly unusual in a French kitchen.

"What is it that is of most value to you here?" I ask Sébastien Bras, a handsome man with an easy smile.

"The relationship we have to Aubrac," he says. "A tradition, a certain light."

At lunch, that light, pale and beautiful, fills the restaurant, which is cantilevered over the plateau of Aubrac, giving diners the impression that they are in

Restaurant Bras, near Laguiole.

A medley of seasonal vegetables — the gargouillou — *is one of chef Michel Bras's signature dishes.*

a sleek and calm spaceship hovering above the countryside. The meal begins with the *gargouillou*, a symphonic poem of textures, colors, and tastes. I believe I will remember this extraordinary pleasure forever, if only for the contrast between the complexity of its preparation and the exquisite simplicity of its final presentation. Every detail of the meal and the environment is surprising and nuanced and, incidentally, also adds up to an object lesson in the passionate regionalism of old Aveyron families like the Brases. So much here, on and around the plates, speaks of the place and its traditions, down to the graceful knives for which Laguiole is famous, the chair legs in the shape of bull horns, the waiters gliding about in blue farmers' smocks.

Véronique Bras mentions a great view near the hotel, so when I leave that afternoon, I continue up the road that climbs the mountain. The plan is only to drive through, but after about 15 minutes, I stop the car and get out: I see now why the plateau of Aubrac is often described as lunar. The vista seems otherworldly, illimitable, sci-fi, shimmering slightly in the extraordinary silence. Here, somehow, time seems actualized, accounted for, and expressed by the eloquent layers of soil, ages ago combining and recombining metamorphic rock, granite, and lava — debris torn from the mountain and carried down by glaciers to the high plain where now almost 2,000 species of plants grow.

I can only get myself back in the car by promising myself, like a child, that I can return. But I just want to see how far up the road goes. It is miles between hamlets. Now the only dwellings are *burons*, and

then suddenly I see the remnants of a monastery: La Dômerie d'Aubrac, built as a refuge for medieval pilgrims. During winter's terrible blizzards, when the winds called *tourmentes* made the snow whirl so densely that paths became invisible, the bell would ring without stop to guide those who were lost and in fear of bandits, wolves, or death from the cold.

Farther up, there are no more houses and no more road, just the *drailles*, the paths made by cattle ascending to high pastures for the summer and descending in autumn. There is no sound at all, except the wind on the mountain. By now, I am completely smitten with this mysterious landscape. The most mysterious thing about it is why everyone isn't here. "Not everybody gets it," Bruno da Silva said to me a day earlier. "Sometimes people come here and they drive up to the plateau and then they come back and say to me, 'But there's nothing there.' How can I answer them? What is nothing for them is everything for us."

Aubrac to Conques is the route that was followed about 1,000 years ago by pilgrims walking across Europe to Galicia, now in Spain, where relics of the apostle James are said to be buried. At the high point of medieval religious fervor, millions of pilgrims traversed the Pyrenees on foot each year. (Even now, 80,000 walk the road of Santiago de Compostela on foot, and 20,000 travel it by other means.) Conques was a major stop, because of the abbey and its raison d'être: a fragment from the skull of the fourth-century martyr Ste. Foy, who was tried by the Romans for refusing to renounce Christianity and condemned to be cooked on a bronze grill and decapitated. Much of the countryside is unchanged since then, and the same road winds down to the village of Conques, curling like a snail shell around the abbey at the bottom. You walk the same narrow streets, pause at the travelers' fountain, and look up, as they must have, at the abbey's glorious tympanum, depicting the Last Judgment. Heaven and hell still seem more divine and horrendous, respectively, than anything you have ever imagined. Angels push back sinners trying to escape. All the way at the bottom, the damned are shoved into the monstrous jaws of hell.

Before they set forth on the journey that would ensure the forgiveness of all their sins, pilgrims took a vow of poverty and gave their fortunes to Conques's abbey. This must have seemed like quite a good deal, based on the tympanum's jaws of hell.

The village of Najac and its
12th-century château.

It's possible to think of the pilgrimages through Aveyron
in the High Middle Ages as Western culture's first
organized tours

The medieval
village of Belcastel.

Nobles, too, made sure that gold and jewels accumulated in the abbey, a masterpiece of Romanesque architecture with its amazingly high dome and its famous "flying tribunes"—galleries on either side that seem suspended just below the ceiling. It can be visited top to bottom. In the evening, at around nine, without warning, the monks begin their chanting by candlelight, an unforgettable spectacle, as it must have been a thousand years ago.

It's even possible to think of the pilgrimages in the High Middle Ages as Western culture's first organized tours, and the apogee of tourism and wealth for the Rouergue. It all went downhill after the Black Plague and the Reformation stanched the flow of devotees. The population shrank: a town like Conques, where 3,000 people lived in the heyday of the pilgrims, has dwindled over time to 300. Even the Industrial Revolution could not stir the impoverished countryside—the windswept pastures, the half-ruined châteaux, the ancient villages, and the one-room farms have all remained intact, left alone behind the mountains for much of the 19th and 20th centuries.

In a way, Aveyron leaped from the Middle Ages directly into the 21st century with the Millau Viaduct. Now the economy seems to be awakening, as some farmers' collectives are thriving by combining modern and traditional techniques, but luckily, Aveyron's revival, if it is one, is being cautiously conducted, guided by tenacious regionalism, pride, know-how, and tremendous respect for nature and history. That's why, as disparate as they seem, you get both Conques and the Viaduct in the *gargouillou*.

On my way out of town, I spot a little shack of a pizzeria, high up on the road above the abbey. For the price of a Coca-Cola I sit and look out at the valley below, fields and churches and turreted castles unchanged since the days when devils and angels vied for popularity with talking cats in boots who made their masters rich.

Sometimes I worry about Aveyron. One day, I eat at a table outside a crêperie in Najac (one of the Most Beautiful Villages), with a lush ravine on my right, and, 100 feet or so up the hill, a 12th-century fortress looming fantastically high above the town. On my left, medieval streets slope down to the river. At the next table, two Englishmen are talking property. "Great buys," one is saying, "the best for the money in the south of France." This jibes all too

neatly with most of the articles I had found online before coming here, the British press touting the region for its real estate potential.

But the next day, I eat my second-best lunch of the year, at the Hôtel-Restaurant du Vieux Pont, in Belcastel—yet another Most Beautiful Village surmounted by yet another stupendous fortress, this one dating back to the 11th century (beating Najac's by 100 years) and still complete with four towers, a drawbridge, and a moat. While I watch the Aveyron River flow under a 500-year-old bridge, it occurs to me: at worst, tourists will continue to cause the occasional summertime traffic jam in the bigger cities like Rodez or Millau, or camp by the dozens in brightly colored tents on the more picturesque mountainsides. For all the eagerness of the *offices de tourisme*, most of the land here is carefully protected: the pastures by the steadfast farmers, the great canyons and plateaus by their status as national parks. The scale has remained entirely human. The Brases' restaurant and hotel are booked months ahead of time, but innumerable charming places to eat and stay are not. I had reserved a table at the restaurant of the Hôtel du Vieux Pont with only a week's notice, though I had not been able to book a room for the night; there are only seven in the hotel—an old village house just on the other side of the bridge—all of them lovely and freshly renovated, and each with a view of the river. Indeed, I made a mental note for my return to Aveyron: *Absolutely spend a night at the Hôtel du Vieux Pont.* My list of such notes was already very long.

The Millau Viaduct, Norman Foster's cable-stayed bridge across the Tarn River Valley.

Millau is a smaller, more gracious southern city than Rodez, and any of the hotels and *chambres d'hôtes* in town or nearby villages put you 10 to 20 minutes' drive by car from irresistible sites and pleasures. Once the world capital of fine glove making (there are still ateliers here that furnish the haute-couture houses), Millau now claims the title of world capital of hang gliding. I cannot report firsthand knowledge of that pursuit, but I can testify that a tour of the nearby Caves of Roquefort will turn you into a lover of Roquefort cheese if you aren't one already. There are boat rides on the Tarn River that pass under the colossal bridge of Millau, with cormorants and herons flying close by for company. You can also visit the archaeological site at La Graufesenque, where the Gauls made the pottery now housed in the Musée Fenaille, or an insect park called Micropolis, or engage in every manner of outdoor adventure in the local rivers and gorges — canoeing, kayaking, swimming, rafting, climbing, rappelling, and riding ponies, horses, and camels. My favorite spectator activity is the rope circuits among the trees in the canyons. Wearing a halter, one delighted or petrified tourist after another leaps like a life-size puppet from one tree to the next.

The highlight of my stay in Millau — perhaps of all of my travels through Aveyron — is a bloodcurdling drive on the road above the gorges of the Tarn River. The road is sometimes so close to the edge that if you look out your window you might think you've taken off; far, far below, the Tarn flows

sometimes gently, sometimes wildly. On the other bank is a bald limestone cliff topped by odd rock formations that seem to tell a story one almost knows. On this day the sky is an unearthly pale blue, cloudless, a playground for eagles and falcons. This is a landscape so exciting and crazy it evokes emotions verging on the operatic. Of course, I realize for the first time: Passion comes from nature.

When I spot the Grand Hôtel de la Muse et du Rozier, nestled at the bottom of a gorge, I feel like throwing away my list of Places to Return to. All of these vistas function like children's-book illustrations, making you gaze and daydream of what it might be like to enter this or that magic place. It turns out there is an infinite number of magic places to get to. So, after a while, one is brimming with curiosity. But perhaps this is what *se ressourcer* feels like.

On my last day, I stayed just outside of Rodez in a renovated château called L'Hostellerie de Fontanges. I need not tell you that it was old, nor that it was charming. In the late afternoon it was warm enough to swim in the pool, then lie down on a chaise longue, daydream, and grow delightfully sleepy. It occurred to me that this was the first day in the two weeks I had spent in Aveyron that I had merely relaxed. I needed to change for dinner — fully expecting a divine meal — but was reluctant to go upstairs, to begin the end of my trip. How many different roads could I have taken?

There is too much variety in Aveyron for a tidy itinerary. But whatever it may lack in dramatic unity it compensates for in pleasure. It really doesn't matter where you begin or end your journey. What matters is the waterfall or the Gothic monastery; the 2,000-year-old bridge or the megalithic tomb where two dusty roads meet; the moment when, at the top of a deserted mountain road, there's a shack with a sign reading CHEZ PIERRE. Just around the next bend, there's a little old hotel; you decide to spend the night. Dinner is served on a cliffside terrace. If you can get yourself to lean over the edge, you'll see the river hundreds of feet below, a few kayaks floating downstream like flowers. You eat side by side with mountain climbers, medievalists, and botanists, and maybe a few glam cosmopolites who stay at the table and talk until very late, drinking local wine. Sometimes laughter drifts up from the river. Sometimes, as if by plan, the diners pause in their various conversations and gaze out at the mountaintops, or down into the irresistible void.

The Tarn River gorge.

The headquarters of Forge de Laguiole, where the renowned knives are made.

Travelers' Guide to Aveyron

WHEN TO GO
Fall and spring in Aveyron bring heavenly weather and few crowds. But in summer, the water sports and hiking are just as enticing.

GETTING THERE
Fly to London or Paris and catch one of the daily connecting flights or the train to Rodez. Or take the high-speed train (TGV) from Paris to Montpellier, and rent a car for the 1½-hour drive to Millau, which takes you over the town's famous viaduct.

GETTING AROUND
Plan to drive, bike, or hike between villages; in the more bucolic areas there is little in the way of bus or taxi service.

EXPLORING AROUND AVEYRON
The Cantal mountains rise to the north of the fertile Vallée du Lot. To the west are the sweltering plains of Montauban and the cool wooded hills of the Gorges de l'Aveyron. In the east lie the arid limestone plateaus of the Grands Causses, and the spectacular gorges carved out by the Tarn River.

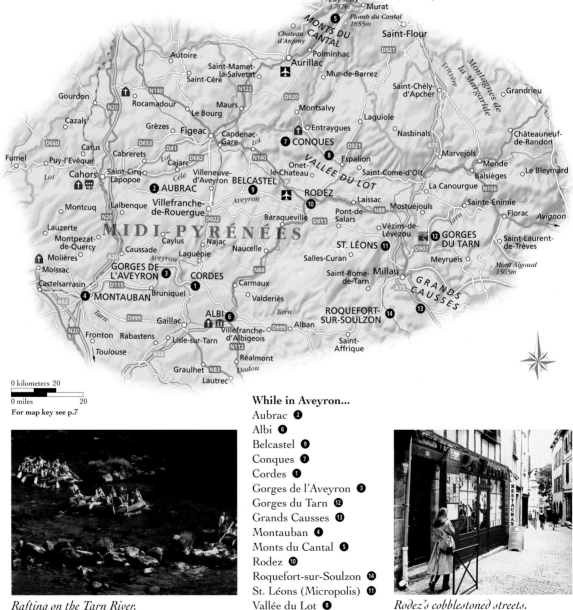

0 kilometers 20

0 miles 20

For map key see p.7

Rafting on the Tarn River.

While in Aveyron...

Aubrac ❷
Albi ❻
Belcastel ❾
Conques ❼
Cordes ❶
Gorges de l'Aveyron ❸
Gorges du Tarn ⑫
Grands Causses ⑬
Montauban ❹
Monts du Cantal ❺
Rodez ⑩
Roquefort-sur-Soulzon ⑭
St. Léons (Micropolis) ⑪
Vallée du Lot ❽

Rodez's cobblestoned streets.

WHERE TO STAY AND EAT

Aveyron has scores of wonderful hotels that also house noteworthy restaurants. These are just a few.

Grand Hôtel de la Muse et du Rozier
Mostuéjouls;
33-5/65-62-60-01;
hotel-delamuse.fr;
doubles from [$][$];
dinner for two [$][$][$].

L'Hostellerie de Fontanges
Rte. de Conques et de Marcillac, Onet-le-Château;
33-5/65-77-76-00;
hostellerie-fontanges.com;
doubles from [$];
dinner for two [$][$].

Hôtel-Restaurant Château de Creissels
A 12th-century château with 30 dreamy rooms, some with balconies over the gardens, others looking out over the Millau Viaduct.
Rte. de St.-Affrique, Millau;
33-5/65-60-16-59;
chateau-de-creissels.com;
doubles from [$],
dinner for two [$][$].

Hôtel-Restaurant Bras
Reserve months in advance.
Rte. de l'Aubrac, Laguiole;
33-5/65-51-18-20;
michel-bras.com;
doubles from [$][$][$];
dinner for two [$][$][$][$].

Hôtel-Restaurant du Vieux Pont
Belcastel;
33-5/65-64-52-29;
hotelbelcastel.com;
doubles from [$];
dinner for two [$][$][$].

Le Comptoir d'Aubrac
Fashion designer Catherine Painvin fled Paris for the Himalayas and finally ended up in Aubrac. The inn, with only six rooms—each more eccentric and wonderful than the last—is a favorite of connoisseurs.
Aubrac;
33-5/65-48-78-84;
catherinepainvincouture.com;
doubles from [$][$];
dinner for two [$][$][$].

Les Demeures de Longcol
A medieval hamlet-turned-hotel in a 54-acre park high above the Aveyron River. Even the pool has a fantastic view.
Najac;
33-5/65-29-63-36;
longcol.com;
doubles from [$][$];
dinner for two [$][$][$].

WHERE TO SHOP

Aveyron's famous **Laguiole knives** can be bought at the new factory, designed by Philippe Starck, at the edge of the village of Laguiole (Rte. de l'Aubrac; 33-5/65-48-43-34; forge-de-laguiole.com). For fine handmade leather gloves, ask at **Musée de Millau** (Hôtel de Pégayrolles, Place Foch, Millau; 33-5/65-59-01-08) for information about local ateliers.

WHAT TO DO

There is no good giudebook to Aveyron in English, so you'll want to rely on tourism offices for both advance and on-the-ground planning, not just for additional sights and hotels but also for sports outfitters of all kinds. They can show you how to follow the **pilgrims' road** to Saint Jacques de Compostelle, for example, a route that includes the magnificent **abbey in Conques**. Many castles and fortresses offer tours. In Paris, contact **Maison de l'Aveyron** (33-1/42-36-84-63; maison-aveyron.org). If you're researching online, try the **Comité Départemental du Tourisme de l'Aveyron** (tourisme-aveyron.com); their site will also provide a list and interactive map of the region's **Most Beautiful Villages of France** (a designation made by a historical preservation association of the same name). The two biggest centers for **outdoor sports** are Millau and Najac.

Caves of Roquefort
Roquefort-sur-Soulzon;
33-5/65-58-54-38;
roquefort-societe.com.

Micropolis City of Insects
St.-Léons;
33-5/65-58-50-50;
micropolis.biz.

Millau Viaduct
Office du Tourisme de Millau, 1 Place du Beffroi, Millau;
33-5/65-60-02-42;
ot-millau.fr.

Musée Fenaille
14 Place Raynaldi, Rodez;
33-5/65-73-84-30;
musee-fenaille.com.

Site Archéologique de la Graufesenque
Millau;
33-5/65-60-11-37.

The bell tower of the Abbaye de Ste.-Foy, at Conques.

Glories of the Loire

FIVE DAYS OF WALKING ALONG GARDEN PATHS AND TREKKING THROUGH FOREST ARE CROWNED BY NIGHTS IN THE MAGNIFICENT CHÂTEAUX OF THE MOST ROMANTIC RIVER VALLEY IN FRANCE. BY FRANK ROSE

We were in the middle of the woods when I began to comprehend the French passion for order. My wife and I were walking through the gently undulating farm country of Berry, on the upper reaches of the Loire. We had just driven down from Paris (two hours on the autoroute) and were expecting fairy-tale *châteaux*, rambles through the countryside, maybe a bit of history: Joan of Arc, the Renaissance court of Francois I… But here we were in the Bois de Cléfy, surrounded by a dense grove of chestnut and oak, standing in a grassy circle from which radiated a half-dozen arrow-straight walkways.

Perfect symmetry. Classicism amid the trees. What struck me was how magical it all was—the crazy sense of rationalism run amok. Only later did I realize that in this clearing I'd stumbled across the essence of France. Order, reason, fairy tales, France itself—all emerged from the Loire Valley during the chaos of the Hundred Years' War. In 1428, when Joan of Arc journeyed to Chinon to convince the dauphin to let her lead an army against the English invaders, the region was home to a wandering royal court about to be overwhelmed by its vassals— one of whom happened to be Henry VI, king of England. A century later, when François I restored

Chambord is the largest of the châteaux in the Loire Valley.

Paris as the capital, this feeble government had evolved into an absolute monarchy ruling all of France. A century and a half after that, the Loire was a sylvan backwater, its deep forests and turreted castles remembered in the fairy tales told at Versailles—worldly parables like "Sleeping Beauty" and "Little Red Riding Hood" that had a moral at the end, the better to enlighten you with.

The next morning we ate breakfast at the 15th-century Château de la Verrerie, where we were staying, in a salon overflowing with ruffled tulips and purple lilacs. Our hostess, the Comtesse Béraud de Vogüé, offered to show us the rest of the château. In her gray pleated skirt and navy cardigan, the countess was the perfect complement to her husband, who'd stridden past earlier in a tweed jacket and hunting boots, a black Lab at his heels. Though his family bought the estate in 1842, she explained, it dates to 1422. In the stone chapel, faded frescoes of the apostles adorned the walls; outside, a witch's hat of a steeple loomed ominously over the gravel courtyard.

Later, as we were packing to go, the count showed me the best route to Chambord, the grandiose hunting lodge built by Francois I in a walled forest. Leaving the *pays fort*, the hilly "strong country" of Berry, we would drive 50 miles across the *pays faible*, the "weak country" of the Sologne. A flat expanse of piney woods and sandy soil, bleak except during a few weeks of autumn color, the Sologne is known for its strawberries, white asparagus, wild boar, and marvelous chèvre.

The spiral staircase at Chambord, built during the reign of François I.

Following the count's directions, we arrived at Chambord on a road that cut straight through the trees to reveal, perfectly centered, the massive towers and fantastical turrets of the château.

That evening we sat surrounded by gilt and silk as the muddy Loire, swollen by two months of relentless spring rains, surged against its banks outside. Our hotel room at Le Choiseul, in the medieval town of Amboise, seemed a good spot to refine our itinerary. The visit to Chambord had been extraordinary, but a lot of friends had told us they'd come to the Loire only to end up chasing tour buses from one château to another. The valley has too many châteaux anyway; to attempt them all is to miss what makes it special—modest vineyards that have produced superb wines for centuries, platoons of white-jacketed waiters bearing tray after tray of tiny delicacies, the sense of order and humanism you might expect of the region that produced both Descartes and Rabelais. Far better to explore it on foot, we figured, and on our own terms—and if a *monument historique* presented itself, so much the better.

After dinner in Le Choiseul's formal restaurant, we ventured out to the quay and saw the town— built, like most here in the Touraine, from the local limestone known as tufa—glowing white in the moonlight beneath the sheer stone walls of its château. The Loire is an aqueous region, adrift on its rivers—the Cher, the Indre, the Vienne, the Loir, the Loire itself. But its fabled *douceur*, the sweetness of its green fields and fertile soil and languid streams, is deceptive. Despite its bounty, this is a strangely mutable place, its skies unpredictable, its rivers untamed, its history capricious and violent. Take the Château d'Amboise, built as a fortress and transformed into a royal palace by Charles VIII, a vigorous and promising monarch who died at 28 after striking his head on a low beam. Today, little remains beyond the apartments he built in the late 15th century, a broad ramp designed to hold armored horsemen, and an exquisitely ornamented Gothic chapel poised on the ramparts, which for a memorable few days in 1560 were hung with the heads and carcasses of rebellious Huguenots.

The next morning in the shadow of the château, we picked up a baguette at a local bakery and, at a nearby charcuterie, discovered rillettes—a wonderfully funky spread of shredded, preserved pork—that has been cooked over a wood fire, as it has been in this region for centuries. Then we headed off through

town to the Forêt d'Amboise, about three miles away. On Rue Victor-Hugo, a narrow street lined with half-timbered tufa houses backed by limestone cliffs, we saw windows cut into the rock itself, trimmed with prim lace curtains on the inside and draped luxuriantly with wisteria on the outside. At a dip in the road we came to the Clos Lucé, the fortified brick mansion where, at the invitation of young François I, Leonardo da Vinci spent the last three years of his life.

Leonardo was one of the spoils of war: no sooner had the French defeated the English in 1453 than they launched a series of fruitless military adventures in Italy that exposed them to the civilizing influence of the Renaissance. While the results can be seen at Chambord, parts of which were designed by Leonardo, they are even more apparent at the Château de Chenonceau, six miles southeast of Amboise, which we visited the following day. Built in the early 1500's by a financier of François I, it was transformed a half-century later into a pleasure palace on the Cher—first by Diane de Poitiers, mistress to Henri II, and then by his widow, Catherine

The Pagode de Chanteloup, a folly at the edge of the forest outside Amboise.

de Médicis, who evicted Diane after his death. The only suggestion that it might once have been a fortress is a vestigial keep, marooned in a forecourt, that now houses a gift shop. Otherwise it is protected by water, not by walls: you encounter a moated forest, then the moated gardens, the moated forecourt, and finally the château itself, bridging the Cher.

During the Second World War, Chenonceau's strategic location—facing occupied France on the right bank of the river, its rear doors opening onto Vichy France on the left bank—made it an ideal escape hatch. But what the Nazis couldn't do, the weather had. A sign at the end of the castle's gallery said that for "security reasons"—heavy rains had brought the Cher to its highest level in 13 years— the rear entrance was closed. We looked out the windows at the massive stone piers supporting the gallery, the muddy waters swirling crazily around them. The path on the left bank seemed passable. Why not try it?

We drove a mile or so downriver, crossed a stone bridge, and parked. The path was a dirt road lined with buttercups, a wheat field on one side, the river and flotsam on the other. Dodging puddles and muck, we made our way back upstream toward Chenonceau. Just beyond the château, we took a trail that veered into the woods. Fifty yards farther on, we found ourselves in a grove of tender young poplars arrayed in perfect rows, their pale green leaves shimmering above us. A light wind blew through the trees, the air sang with bird calls, and as we headed back to the river the sun emerged, turning the pale gray château a dazzling, glorious white.

The best way to experience the legendary white limestone of the Touraine, it turns out, is to sleep in it. Just outside Tours, in Rochecorbon, one of the more luxurious cave dwellings in France has been carved from the cliffs above the Loire. It's a hotel called Les Hautes Roches, and as you drive through the gates the rocks loom directly overhead. Our room had smoothly articulated walls, as if they'd been built of stone rather than excavated from it, and a faint mineral smell. Otherwise, only the rough-hewn ceiling and the depth of the window wells suggested that we were actually inside the earth.

A mile down the road is the village of Vouvray, known for its Chenin Blancs. Like most Loire wines, Vouvrays are simple and unpretentious. The town seemed simple enough, too: a couple of narrow streets lined with modest shops, a church, some neatly kept houses. Parking our rented Renault at a quiet intersection, we headed for the vineyards on foot. The road took us up past the cliffs to a wide

*Château de Chenonceau's perfectly
groomed park and elegant gardens
were originally commissioned in the
16th century by Diane de Poitiers,
mistress to Henri II.*

The Château de Chenonceau, which lies near the small village of Chenonceaux, is built right over the Cher river.

plateau planted with vines. We found ourselves beneath a threatening sky, its towering clouds black and spitting raindrops one moment, peaceful the next. At one point a rainbow appeared, then vanished almost immediately. Here and there the road would pass old farmhouses surrounded by spring flowers — tulips, pansies, hyacinths, and peonies. We'd been walking a couple of hours when, at the outskirts of a hamlet called Le Grand Ormeau, we saw a sign in the middle of the vineyard: CHAMPALOU.

Didier Champalou is among the premier wine makers of Vouvray. Entering a walled yard, we found a workman in the barn — an athletic-looking man with deep-blue eyes: Champalou himself. Although he clearly wasn't set up for tastings (they can be arranged by appointment), he insisted on fetching some glasses from the house. The wines he poured grew more and more intense — first a *méthode champenoise*, then a dry white, then a semi-dry, then a sweet *moelleux* — until finally he pulled out his '96 Trie de Vendange. It was a heady wine, richly honeyed, ambrosial on the tongue, and as complex and layered as the Loire itself.

Dinner that evening was at Jean Bardet, in Tours's 19th-century St.-Symphorien district. Bardet's Château Belmont is a white tufa mansion set amid emerald lawns: inside, creamy yellow dining rooms are set off by spectacular bouquets of anthuriums and white lilacs. Bardet's cooking offers a forward-thinking menu — heaps of fresh herbs, stocks in place of cream, that sort of thing — not lacking for conceits. Baby eel was glorious in its sauce of red Bourgueil wine; white asparagus topped with a poached egg and crisped Parmesan, even more so. We returned to Les Hautes Roches to discover a light dusting of limestone on the bureaus. It's easier to rationalize a forest, apparently, than the earth itself.

The next day we drove to Chinon, a river town squeezed between the Vienne and the craggy heights that support its château. A few miles away, at the northern edge of the Fôret de Chinon, is the château that's supposed to have inspired Charles Perrault's "Sleeping Beauty." In the fairy tale, the sleeping princess's castle is hidden in a forest so thick with trees and brambles that only the tops of its turrets can be seen. In reality the forest seemed dark and more than a little desolate — the trees almost stunted, the few buildings we could see apparently abandoned. We left our car by a half-ruined barn and started walking.

The snow-white inhabitants of a farm in Chenonceaux, some 16 miles east of Tours.

We passed an overgrown cherry orchard, and just beyond it, a stone farmhouse that hadn't been occupied in decades, its barns empty and forlorn. We'd been walking for an hour when the woods broke and we found ourselves in the tidy village of Rigny-Ussé. Soon we were staring up at the Château d'Ussé, whose terraced gardens and gleaming turrets stood in sharp relief against the deeply wooded hillsides behind it. At its feet, another road set off across the marshy Indre to the Loire. We continued walking, turning back from time to time to see the view: the pastoral farmland between the rivers, the forbidding forest rising above it, and in the middle the château, a magical hinge between the tamed and the wild. Sleeping Beauty's castle or not, it certainly looked the part.

We had one final walk mapped out: from l'Abbaye de Fontevraud, the 12th-century royal abbey a few miles west of Chinon, across the wheat fields to Candes-St.-Martin. Though the abbey is as extensive as most royal châteaux, its location in a

51

fold in the hills gives it the appearance of humility. From the village you go down to Fontevraud, and the farther you descend the more extraordinary it becomes. Finally, beneath a soaring Romanesque nave, you encounter the polychrome death effigies of England's Plantagenet rulers—Henry II and his queen, Eleanor of Aquitaine, their son Richard the Lion-Hearted at their feet. And it hit me that if it hadn't been for Joan of Arc, the United Kingdom would probably consist of England, Wales, Scotland, and France.

A major hiking trail, the GR3, passes near the abbey. We followed it into the woods and took a farm road from there to Candes-St.Martin, a mile or

A 16th-century windmill,
in Turquant.

so farther on. The road had already begun to drop sharply toward the Loire when a sudden bend brought us to a cobblestoned square. At its center stood the 12th-century Church of St.-Martin, a shrine to the Roman centurion who gave his cloak to a beggar and ended up as bishop of Tours. The church was small but majestic, with vaulted ceilings, brilliant stained glass, and—more unusually—crenellated towers, added during the Hundred Years' War to defend it from attackers.

It was late afternoon when we left Candes-St.-Martin, and we still had to walk back to Fontevraud. The sky, which had been gray all day, began to spatter us with rain. We were due that evening at the Château de Noirieux, a Relais & Châteaux hotel outside Angers, which looked to be about an hour-and-a-half's drive. I had a vague recollection of being told that the château's gates closed at 10, and no memory at all of where I might have written down the code to get in.

As the abbey church at Fontevraud came into view across the ravine, the trail turned steep. Slipping downhill, we arrived at Fontevraud chilled, sweaty, and smeared with mud. But there was no time to wash up and no place to do it anyway, so we drove across the Loire, picked up the autoroute, and pointed our Renault toward Angers.

It was 8:55 when we pulled up to the château. In the fading light we could make out the river Loir overflowing its banks below us. Yet the grandly proportioned château, with its balustraded terraces, its terra-cotta epergnes brimming with pansies, its poplars in perfect rows, conveyed a reassuring sense of civilization, which we were definitely ready for.

My French, none too good at the best of times, failed me completely in my exhaustion, but the desk clerk didn't mind: "You can speak English now, sir," she said helpfully. Meanwhile, bellhops materialized. Bags were carried off. As the car disappeared, we were ushered to a gabled room in the manor house. A half hour later, freshly scrubbed, we made our way to the restaurant, which was still busy enough to feel festive. We slept late the next morning, so late that the restaurant was closed when we went down for breakfast. No matter: waiters started carrying furniture into the bar and set up a table for us there. As we sipped our coffee, my wife told me about the dream she'd had: how we had set out on a hike and found at every crossroads a waiter from Noirieux bearing bottles of Perrier, or a delightful little snack, or a beautifully wrapped set of directions for the next stage of our trip. I had to admit, it did sound like the way to travel.

For all its bounty, the Loire is a strangely mutable place, its skies unpredictable, its rivers untamed, its history capricious and violent

Poppies in a roadside field near the 12th-century Abbaye de Fontevraud.

Travelers' Guide to the Loire Valley

GETTING THERE

Nantes-Atlantique Airport is served by flights from most European cities, as well as from Montreal. Alternatively, fly to Paris and pick up a connecting flight to Nantes or Tours. Chartres, Le Mans, Angers, and Nantes are reached from Paris by the A11 autoroute. The A10 links Orléans, Blois, and Tours. By rail, Tours is one hour on the TGV, and Nantes is two hours.

EXPLORING THE LOIRE VALLEY

The lush landscape, studded with France's finest châteaux, is the main attraction. Peaceful country breaks can be had in the Loire and Indre valleys, and in the Vendée, while the sandy Atlantic coast is ideal for beach vacations. Wine tours focus on Bourgueil, Chinon, Muscadet, Saumur, and Vouvray bottlings. The most charming bases are Amboise, Blois, Beaugency, and Saumur.

Château de Chaumont.

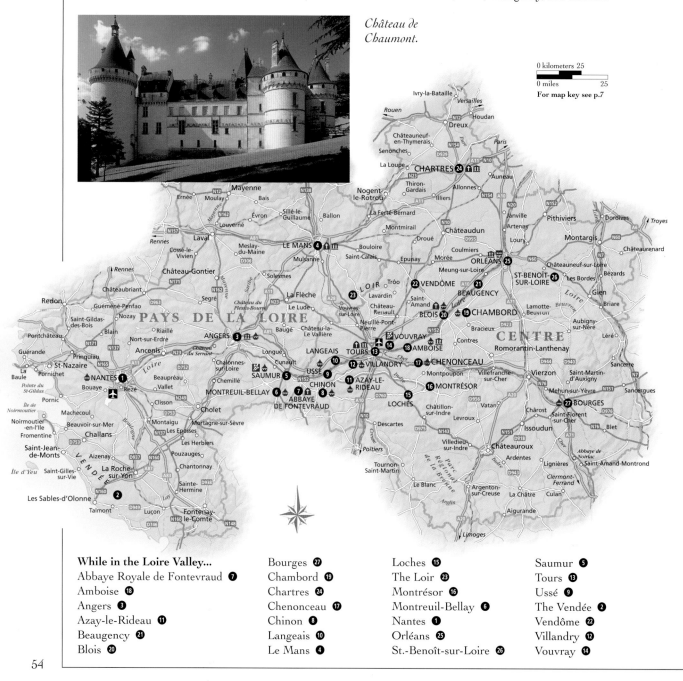

0 kilometers 25

0 miles 25

For map key see p.7

While in the Loire Valley...

Abbaye Royale de Fontevraud ❼	Bourges ㉗	Loches ⓯	Saumur ❺
Amboise ⓲	Chambord ⓳	The Loir ㉓	Tours ⓭
Angers ❸	Chartres ㉔	Montrésor ⓰	Ussé ❾
Azay-le-Rideau ⓫	Chenonceau ⓱	Montreuil-Bellay ❻	The Vendée ❷
Beaugency ㉑	Chinon ❽	Nantes ❶	Vendôme ㉒
Blois ⓴	Langeais ❿	Orléans ㉕	Villandry ⓬
	Le Mans ❹	St.-Benoît-sur-Loire ㉖	Vouvray ⓮

WHERE TO STAY

Château de la Verrerie
A Scottish-style castle in the heart of France.
Oizon,
33-2/48-81-51-60;
ila-chateau.com;
doubles from $$

Le Choiseul
An 18th-century compound on the Loire, with the Château d'Amboise rising behind.
36 Quai Charles-Guinot, Amboise;
33-2/47-30-45-45;
slh.com;
doubles from $$

Les Hautes Roches
Charming cave dwelling overlooking the Loire just outside Tours.
86 Quai de la Loire, Rochecorbon;
33-2/47-52-88-88;
leshautesroches.com;
doubles from $$

Château de Noirieux
A 17th-century château made over in the 1920's as a luxurious country house, only to be made over again as an even more luxurious hotel.
26 Rte. du Moulin, Briollay;
33-2/41-42-50-05;
chateaudenoirieux.com;
doubles from $$

WHERE TO EAT

Restaurant La Tour
Luminous 14th-century spot in a town whose name is synonymous with a delicious Sauvignon Blanc.
31 Nouvelle Place, Sancerre;
33-2/48-54-00-81;
dinner for two $$

La Maison d'Hélène
Marvelous country cooking in a half-timbered cottage in the park of the château.

Château de la Verrerie, Oizon;
33-2/48-58-24-27;
dinner for two $$$

Hôtel du Bon Laboureur et du Château
Ivy-covered inn whose specialties include braised veal sweetbreads.
6 Rue du Docteur Bretonneau, Chenonceaux;
33-2/47-23-90-02;
dinner for two $$$

Jean Bardet Château Belmont
A temple of gastronomy, with twenty-one guest rooms—the best lodging in Tours (doubles from $$).
57 Rue Grison, Tours;
33-2/47-41-41-11;
dinner for two $$$$

Au Plaisir Gourmand
In an old house hidden in a tiny courtyard, Jean-Claude Rigollet artfully balances the earthy with the refined.
2 Rue Parmentier, Chinon;
33-2/47-93-20-48;
dinner for two $$$

WHERE TO SHOP

Charcuterie Hardouin
Meaty rillettes, ethereal spinach-and-salmon quiche, and rice salad studded with mussels and squid.
25 Rte. Nationale 152, Vouvray;
33-2/47-52-60-24.

Vignoble Champalou
Vouvray's best producers do wonders with Chenin Blanc, and Champalou's are extraordinary, especially his moelleux .
7 Rue du Grand-Ormeau, Vouvray;
33-2/47-52-64-49.

Domaine Olga Raffault
Chinon's leading wine maker produces reds that are fruity and delicate.
1 Rue des Caillis Roguinet, Savigny-en-Véron;
33-2/47-58-42-16.

WHAT TO READ

Art and Architecture in France 1500–1700
By Sir Anthony Blunt.
The aesthete's tour of the French Renaissance, with Britain's most notorious spy as your guide.

A Wine and Food Guide to the Loire
By Jacqueline Friedrich.
Essential reading for the discerning gourmand.

Château de Saumur.

PART TWO
Places to Stay

*The Place
Vendôme entrance
to the Paris Ritz.*

Dusk falls on Le Mas des Câpriers's 1897 roulotte, *in Provence.*

Photographs by Benoît Peverelli

On the Wagon

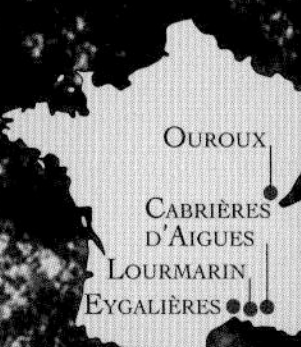

THE GLOBAL YURT CRAZE IS OVER—YOU HADN'T HEARD?—MAKING WAY
FOR REFURBISHED GYPSY *ROULOTTES*, OR CARAVANS, TO BECOME *THE* OUTRÉ
FRENCH ACCOMMODATIONS. BY CHRISTOPHER PETKANAS

OUROUX
CABRIÈRES
D'AIGUES
LOURMARIN
EYGALIÈRES

Whether you view it generously as borrowing or disapprovingly as stealing, France's talent for cherry-picking the domestic *savoir-vivre* of others is hard not to admire. It's no accident that the French word for "cozy" is *cozy*, shorthand for *le style anglais*, an organic cocktail of proudly chipped creamware, cracked-leather fireplace fenders, and squishy chintz sofas. Generations after being introduced, the look has lost none of its potency, succeeding still in making French ladies in velvet headbands and boiled-wool jackets quiver and swoon.

For better or worse, *la cuisine américaine*, which describes an open kitchen that spills into another room, is also here to stay in France, while apartments from Le Mans to Marseilles are stuffed with a souk's worth of embroidered straw mats, mosaic tiles, and hammered-copper platters the size of Humvee hubcaps. (If you had lost Morocco as a colony, you might be nostalgic for this stuff, too.) And I won't soon forget the Hexagon's recent affair with yurts. Something about the typical provincial back garden, with its sighing hollyhocks and regimented lettuces, did not lend itself to fantasies of Kirghiz nomads.

La Romantique,
a roulotte, *at Le*
Mas dou Pastre, in
Eygalières.

60

Inside La Manouche, at Le Mas dou Pastre.

Fashion is cruel. Call it opportunism, or itchiness, or avarice, but the French waste no time moving on. Once they folded those yurts away in the attic to recharge their novelty for the grandkids, they hitched themselves to *roulottes*, or covered Gypsy wagons, and the footloose bohemian esprit that goes with them. Transgression is also part of *roulottes'* appeal, allowing a population with famously conformist (and bourgeois) ideas about taste to express their inner magpie. The interiors of these veritable maisonettes on wheels are not so much borderline kitsch as kitsch. Light the campfire, tune up the violin, put a hedgehog in the oven, and bring on the dancing bears.

From Burgundy to the Bouches-du-Rhône, it seems you can't open an inn these days without a *roulotte* as a piquant alternative to the prosaic *chambre avec douche*. Tucked under trees or planted on well-chosen patches of green, they are used by home owners as guesthouses, offices, salons for reading and napping and taking the evening aperitif, or simply as spare rooms, exotic and transporting. Like mobile homes in France, *roulottes* benefit from the official designation HLL, *Habitation Légère de Loisir*, or Light Leisure Dwelling. As such, they require only parking permits, making them an easy way of

adding square footage to a house or inn without enduring the red tape of an actual build. Anything not to deal with town hall.

Roulottes rolled across my imagination in the early eighties and never left. My enchantment is traceable to a little book called *Pierre Deux's French Country*, that sun-soaked volume about Provençal houses and textiles and pottery that transformed the south of France from an unself-conscious region into a self-conscious religion (500,000 copies in print worldwide). A lovely *roulotte* appears on page 143. This was my first exposure. Like photographs of unclothed people I find attractive, the picture kept me going for a while but then ceased to.

Working for *W* magazine in Paris, I casually contrived to assign myself a story on the founders of Souleiado fabrics, who—don't look at me, I was only doing my job—also happened to own the *roulotte*. With perfect innocence they led me to it, mysterious and melancholy, beside their little farmhouse. Isn't it crazy the things a person can get hooked on?

Roulotte culture is immense. My education had begun. In 1888 van Gogh painted *Encampment of Gypsies with Caravans*, a signal work of his Arles period. In *Madeline and the Gypsies*, Bemelmans has his star schoolgirl join the circus and make a tour

Even the kitchen sink is included in the roulotte at Le Mas des Câpriers.

The foyer of La Manouche.

de France in a *roulotte* ("Gypsies do not like to stay — / They only come to go away"), with postcard stops in front of Chartres cathedral and Mont-St.-Michel. Zola recalled how as a troubled schoolboy he longed to bump along forever in a *roulotte* to nowhere. "He lives as one dreams of living, in a caravan," Cocteau noted of the great Gypsy guitarist Django Reinhardt. "And even when it was no longer a caravan, somehow it still was." Today, *roulottes* are part of the iconography used by the Gipsy Kings, who come from Gypsy communities in Arles and Montpellier, to sell and explain themselves and their rumba flamenca to *gadje*, the often hostile outside world.

Most scholars agree that the Gypsies are an Indian people who left the subcontinent in the 10th century for Persia. From there the exodus continued to Armenia, Syria, the future Iraq, Byzantine Greece, the Balkans, Western Europe, and North America. "The Gypsies have no home," Isabel Fonseca writes in her portrait of contemporary gypsy life, *Bury Me Standing*, "and, perhaps uniquely among peoples, they have no dream of a homeland." Long past World War II, *roulottes* remained a way of life for European Gypsies, serving as both dwellings and conveyances, until government-enforced sedentarization in many countries forced them off the roads. Given their anguished history, some see the fetishization of *roulottes* in France as trivializing and politically insensitive.

Before innkeepers unlocked their romantic potential, the vehicles were tough if not impossible for *gadje* to penetrate. Even before I began restoring an 1814 ruin in Provence in 1994, I'd go out of my way to stop at a *roulotte* that sells olive oil and dried herbs at the entrance to Fontvieille, the village made known by *Lettres de mon moulin*, Alphonse Daudet's humanist masterpiece. I still shop there; my interest in the dusty herbs is feigned, but at least they get me inside. And there is always some fashion lesson to be learned from the owner, who may or may not be a Gypsy and who wears clanking jewelry and a cinched blouse pulled down to expose her shoulders. But the last time I visited she showed what seemed like a dangerous level of admiration for my friend Odile's long and colorful flounced skirt. We both felt that if we lingered any longer in that dark airless room a line might be crossed. "*J'aime ta jupe!*" the woman exclaimed, pulling at the hem. "I love your skirt!"

There are more recycled *roulottes* in Provence than anywhere else in France because the Provençaux have long observed *les gens du voyage*, or travelers, and been students of their customs. Every May, Gypsies from all over the world make the pilgrimage to the Camargue to the whitewashed coastal town of Les Saintes-Maries-de-la-Mer to celebrate their patron saint, Sara. The pilgrims believe that in the first century A.D., Jesus' two aunt Marys, Jacobe and Salome, and their Egyptian servant Sara miraculously crossed the Mediterranean from Jerusalem without a sail, oars, or provisions, landing and ultimately being entombed in Les Saintes. (Actually not everyone agrees that the servant was on board.) During the spring celebration, effigies of Sara, who is depicted as black, and the white Marys, all in festive spangly capes, are held aloft in a procession into the sea. It's a frenetic moment made more so by a splashing convoy of horses.

In the quasi-cryptic realm of second-use *roulottes* in France today, all roads lead to Jeanne Bayol, who chases down vintage examples from England to Estonia, then rehabilitates them in her plein-air atelier in St.-Rémy-de-Provence. An average model, in wood or tole-faced wood, is 20 feet long, has seven-foot ceilings, costs $20,000, and is not capable of doing more than a short turn around the garden.

A view past the ornate woodburner into the bedroom of La Manouche.

63

Le Mas des Câpriers' roulotte, *in Provence, by day.*

spending an onerous night: the *roulotte* is a lot more comfortable than you might think, and you'd be surprised how quickly and naturally you tailor your movements to its constraints). Inside, French doors separate a sitting room and a bedroom with a queen-size bed, both naïvely paneled in oak. Crocheted curtains, long-stemmed cloth roses, a floral patchwork bedcover, an Eiffel tower snow globe, and a crucifix complete the look.

Cloth flowers are lovely, of course, but not strictly necessary, not like, for most of us anyway, a toilet. And hot water. And heating. The *roulotte* has all three. The toilet is retrofitted in a tiny closet. Water flows just like at home, into a porcelain sink. Space heaters chase the chill. Only the shower is outside. What a shower: banged together from the thick, hairy planks of packing crates, the huge alfresco stall is snuggled under a canopy of pines.

Most of us have memories we fear are too cinematic, or too fantastic, or too picturesque to trust. I checked into Câpriers with what I thought was a complete mental inventory of everything I knew about ambulant Gypsy habitats. But by morning I was remembering something additional, the time decades ago when, driving on a back road in the choking heat between Arles and Fontvieille, I saw a *roulotte*, drawn by a lumbering mule, being used the way it was meant to be used, by a Gypsy family on the move.

Bayol's reputation was sealed, and the vogue for *roulottes* informally ignited, when Jacques Grange, a neighbor and the nearest thing the French have to decorating royalty, became one of her first customers. Since then she has supplied *roulottes* to a portfolio of *auberges de charme* in the region, including Le Mas dou Pastre and Le Mas des Câpriers. Les Roulottes de la Serve offers a similar experience in the Beaujolais. And though the *roulottes* at the hotel-restaurant La Fenière, in the Luberon mountains, are new, they follow traditional designs and are made by artisans, Les Roulottiers, in the Midi-Pyrénées. The wagons at most inns are gently priced. Except for Serve, all of the above places also have conventional lodgings.

I'm going to stick my neck out and say that Mas des Câpriers, lost deep in the countryside, has the most arcadian setting of any guesthouse in Provence. Delivered on a flatbed truck, its 1897 *roulotte* is marooned on a rise on the edge of a bosk and attended by cement mushrooms—garden ornaments—daubed with polka dots. A birdcage hangs from the hourglass chassis, beveled windows betray a kind of Art Nouveau wishfulness, and potted pansies line the steps to the front door (where, by the way, you can check your fears about

A cluster of ornamental mushrooms flanks the roulotte at Le Mas des Câpriers.

The roulotte is a lot more comfortable than you might think, and you'd be surprised how quickly and naturally you tailor your movements to its constraints

Travelers' Guide to Provence

GETTING THERE

There is a daily Delta flight from New York to Nice from April through October. You can also fly to Paris and pick up connections to Marseilles, Avignon, and Toulon-Hyères; by rail, the TGV Méditerranée from Paris to Provence leaves from Gare de Lyon.

The summit of Mont Ventoux, in the Mistral season.

While in Provence...
Aix-en-Provence 15
Alpes-Maritimes 41
Antibes 29
Arles 13
Avignon 5
Biot 31
Cagnes-sur-Mer 32
Cannes 27
Cap d'Antibes 28
Cap Ferrat 38
Carpentras 6
Cassis 17
Châteauneuf-du-Pape 4
Digne-les-Bains 23
Èze 39
Fontaine-de-Vaucluse 7
Fréjus 24
Gordes 8
Gorges du Loup 33
Grasse 26
Hyères 19
Îles d'Hyères 20
La Carmargue 14
Les Baux-de-Provence 11
Luberon 9
Marseille 16
Massif des Maures 21
Menton 42
Monaco 43
Mont Ventoux 1
Nice 36
Orange 3
Roquebrune-Cap-Martin 40
St.-Paul-de-Vence 35
St.-Raphaël 25
St.-Rémy-de-Provence 10
St.-Tropez 22
Tarascon 12
Toulon 18
Vaison-la-Romaine 2
Vallauris 30
Vence 34
Villefranche-sur-Mer 37

EXPLORING PROVENCE

The coast of this southeastern region is France's most popular holiday destination. Sun-worshippers flock to the beaches in the summer months, which is also a time for opera, dance, and jazz festivals, bull fights, and boules games. Inland are lavender fields, remote mountain plateaus, precariously perched villages, and dramatic river gorges. The image of Provence bathed in sunshine is marred only when the bitter Mistral wind scours the land, sporadically from December through April.

0 kilometers 25
0 miles 25

For map key see p.7

LES SAINTES-MARIES-DE-LA-MER
Every May, gypsies make a pilgrimage to this fortified church in the Camargue, marking the legendary 1st-century arrival of the saints Mary Salome and Mary Jacobe, and their handmaiden Sarah, the gypsies' patron saint.

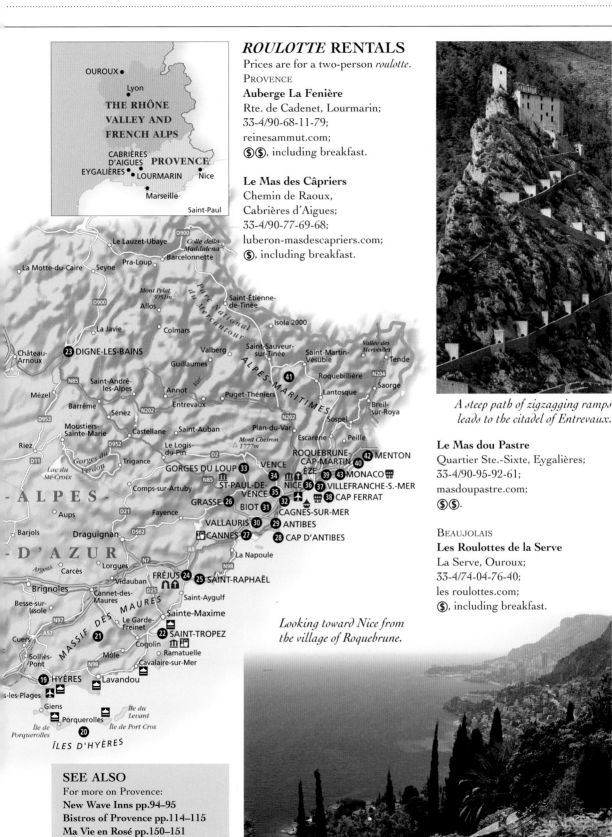

THE RHÔNE VALLEY AND FRENCH ALPS

OUROUX

Lyon

CABRIÈRES D'AIGUES — PROVENCE
EYGALIÈRES • LOURMARIN — Nice
Marseille
Saint-Paul

ROULOTTE RENTALS

Prices are for a two-person *roulotte*.

PROVENCE

Auberge La Fenière
Rte. de Cadenet, Lourmarin;
33-4/90-68-11-79;
reinesammut.com;
$$, including breakfast.

Le Mas des Câpriers
Chemin de Raoux,
Cabrières d'Aigues;
33-4/90-77-69-68;
luberon-masdescapriers.com;
$, including breakfast.

A steep path of zigzagging ramps leads to the citadel of Entrevaux.

Le Mas dou Pastre
Quartier Ste.-Sixte, Eygalières;
33-4/90-95-92-61;
masdoupastre.com;
$$.

BEAUJOLAIS

Les Roulottes de la Serve
La Serve, Ouroux;
33-4/74-04-76-40;
les roulottes.com;
$, including breakfast.

Looking toward Nice from the village of Roquebrune.

Puttin' on the Ritz

HOW DOES THE MOST VENERATED HOTEL IN PARIS KEEP THE SHOW GOING IN AN AGE OF PDA "CONCIERGES," CELEBRITY ENTOURAGES, AND STIFF NEW COMPETITION? BY CHRISTOPHER PETKANAS

PARIS

Just inside the front entrance of the Paris Ritz and steps away from the hotel's Bar Vendôme, home of the $54 lobster club, is a limed-oak door you have no reason to have ever noticed, though your entire happiness as a guest hangs on the decisions made behind it. Should chambermaids be authorized to change the 2.8-ounce bars of soap in the bathrooms, even when you can still see the La Prairie logo? Will hiring a period horse-drawn carriage with attendants in livery to trot people around Place Vendôme on Valentine's Day play into their silliest Paris fantasies, or is it a cheesy stunt best shelved? Has the red Menu Monochrome (prawns in raspberry vinaigrette, beetroot tart with red-pepper *jus*) at L'Espadon, the hotel's restaurant, lost its novelty value, and if so, what should replace it? An all-blue menu would allow executive chef Michel Roth to

Photographs by Andrea Fazzari

blow through a lot of undercooked steak, but what about green? Yellow? Beige? Okay, maybe not beige.

Nail-biting issues like these are weighed at the Ritz seven days a week at 9 a.m. briefings run by Omer Acar, the hotel's amazingly young (he's 37) general manager, and attended by more than a dozen department heads, including lieutenants responsible for guest relations, banqueting, the cooking school, the health club, technical systems like plumbing—even personnel you wouldn't have thought needed to be kept in the loop, like the women in charge of the switchboard and laundry. The thinking behind this MO became clear to me when I took the service elevator "by mistake," hoping to learn something I wasn't supposed to. I didn't hear the question a groom asked a *chasseur*, but when no answer was forthcoming, the groom, clearly drunk on Ritz Kool-Aid, snapped, "*Écoute-moi bien, idiot*. Your business is my business."

But I'm getting ahead of myself.

Two days earlier I'd pulled up to the Ritz, which for sense of arrival nothing can touch. The early 18th-century square it fringes—Place Vendôme, the most famous in Paris—is actually not a square at all, but a subtle octagon watched over by a statue of Napoleon in the drag of a Roman emperor. The architect Jules Hardouin-Mansart achieved a rare harmony by conceiving all the buildings on the *place* as an ensemble: the limestone façades went up first, followed by the town houses behind them.

The hotel's limestone exterior, designed by architect Jules Hardouin-Mansart and built in 1705.

The hotel's celebrated entrance, on Place Vendôme.

Outside the Ritz today there are almost always fans poignantly waiting to snap this or that celebrity. When the star is huge enough—Madonna, for example—a guest can earn a quick 20 euros just by leading a fan under one of the four arches, along a crimson carpet, up three broad steps, and through the revolving door.

One of the Ritz's great triumphs is its stubborn lack of a traditional lobby. Instead you get a long, wide corridor with just a few throne-like perches and towering French windows dressed in a cataclysm of swags and rippling jabots. Typically, the scene is animated by conspicuously American Americans (nearly 40 percent of the hotel's customers are from the United States), looking like deer caught in headlights; Japanese wearing face masks against threats to their hygiene; grungy young couples who may or may not be in the music business; Italians in Loro Piana with poor cell-phone etiquette; and a big-spending new constituency, Ukrainians, that every high-end hotelier in Paris is trying to lure. Anything goes in the corridor lobby: when a pack of English children sat down in the middle of traffic and dumped out their coloring supplies, no one stopped them. Hardly a topic for the morning briefing, but distressing nevertheless.

Held in English, the staccato meetings take place in a squeezed mezzanine-level War Room overlooking Place Vendôme. (If the windows are open and you stand in just the right spot, you can learn that soap replacement is discretionary, the carriage is a yes, and the red menu was retired last fall.) Space is so tight in the War Room, housekeeping might invite human resources to share a chair. Other managers stand, holding up the walls. Not that anyone minds. It's easy to imagine this group sharing anecdotes about their kids, their kids' schools, their lovers, their lovers' wives and husbands.

But not here. A hotel that has no trouble getting $10.40 for an in-room Nespresso pod may sound like it owns the world. But with a salaried population of 526 and an operating budget larger than that of some French towns, the Ritz is feeling the heat of competition more acutely than at any time in its 109-year history. The Mother of All Grand Luxury Hotels is still trying to figure out if there is a place for it in a century that is already 85 months old. And yet if the first step in fixing a problem is admitting you have one, at least the Ritz is no longer in denial. Management finally comprehends that if you're going to call yourself the greatest hotel in the world and charge $950 for a 270-square-foot entry-level room in the Cambon wing (a.k.a. Siberia), you'd better have something to back it up. And wouldn't it be great if that something was relevant, original, fizzy—not just another 25 miles of Houlès passementerie?

In his eagerness to keep the Ritz current and cure its vulnerabilities, Acar can seem to be swatting flies. But the hotel's cocktail of recently added services, distractions, absurdities, temptations, gadgets, indulgences, frivolities, impertinences, and enticements is a potent one. Having hired Pierre-Yves Rochon, who decorated the Four Seasons George V, also in Paris, the Ritz obviously wouldn't mind if a little of that hotel's fairy dust was sprinkled its way. Rochon has swept through the 162 guest rooms, which have been described in *Travel+Leisure* as penitentiaries as imagined by Barbara Cartland, and replaced the beds with an austerely elegant upholstered-and-gilded design, garnished with pinecone finials and fit for a dauphin. Rochon's intervention is a first step toward banishing the faux Frenchiness and petit-four sickliness of his predecessor, Philippe Belloir, but I do question the sateen sheets. They don't seem very...would *modern* be the right word?

But the management's efforts to get the sheets right are nothing compared to the minutiae that preoccupied César Ritz, the hotel's founder. This son of Swiss peasants sought to invest his enterprise with "all the refinements of living that a prince might hope to incorporate in his town house." Ritz is said to be the first hospitality professional to notice that Americans are obsessed with ice water, which he furnished before they asked for it. Recognizing that

there are people who can never make up their minds between a dozen and a half-dozen oysters, he had plates specially made to hold nine. The closet interiors Ritz designed even featured a dedicated drawer for women's hairpieces.

Through the sixties, the hotel introduced *nouveautés* only after agonizing consideration. These days they come fast and furious: send it up the flagpole and see if anyone salutes. New chapters in the Ritz's history are being written with an all-organic room-service menu as well as L'Espadon's vegetarian and monochrome menus (while the first is gastronomically sound, the second never rises above its gimmick). In association with Parfums Thierry Mugler, the Ritz Escoffier cooking school is offering Ateliers Vins, where students isolate the notes in a fragrance (rose and raspberry in Alien for Women, say), then reconjure them in the kitchen (*gelée de rose à la framboise*). This is actually less hokey than it sounds and a terrific way to spend a Friday night in Paris, particularly if you want to meet people. Colin Field evaluates and rejiggers the alcoholic creations of students who sign up for his mixology classes in the snug paneled confines of the Hemingway Bar, which he runs. Field is so entertaining that no one would care if all he did was recount his romantic life as a bartender. As one learns, this has involved a certain number of Moulin Rouge showgirls.

Abstemious and feeling left out? Darjeeling is poured at the Ritz 10 days after harvesting. If your kids are not already brats, lacquered baskets filled with certified-green goodies—a stuffed animal, Bomford baby balm, cotton PJ's—are not going to get them in line. Last year the hotel had the good idea of holding a competition for a new floral designer, though unfortunately I don't think they got the right guy. Djordje Varda, self-taught and from Serbia, is very talented, and I believe he believes in what he is doing. But his spidery, vertical, nose-thumbing compositions are frankly a little scary, and they declare war on a house style that—if you plow through the pastiche and reproductions of reproductions—champions the decorative idioms to which a succession of Louis lent their names. Clumps of catnip, with their turf, posed directly on the odd antique, a marble-topped commode? You could be dreaming. Except you're not.

While pretending that their own innovations and wonderful occupancy rates keep them too busy to notice, the Ritz's rivals in the so-called palace

A daily staff meeting at 9 a.m. in the War Room.

The lobby corridor.

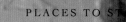

Housekeeping staff at the Ritz.

Polishing the chandelier in the Windsor Suite.

hotel category spend a lot of time tracking such developments, reading them as if they were tea leaves. (Sometimes a crumb of turf is a crumb of turf.) For years the number of Paris palace hotels—an unofficial designation, which the French fetishize but which means little to me and you—was stalled at five, not counting the Ritz: the George V, the Crillon, the Plaza-Athénée, the Meurice, and the Bristol. The Ritz had it easy. If it worried at all, it was about these institutions.

The stakes were raised in 1999 when the George V was reborn and rebranded as a brilliantly polished Four Seasons. It continues to take a big bite out of the Ritz's business—specifically, its American business (Ritz customers are faithful, up to a point). Three years later, the Park Hyatt opened up the block. Humbled by the reaction to all those disturbing Christ-like bronzes commissioned by designer Ed Tuttle, the Hyatt is less insistent on referring to itself as Paris's first modern palace hotel than it was when it launched. In late 2006, Fouquet's Barrière bowed noisily on the Champs-Élysées, calling itself the best this and the best that, though I honestly don't think the Ritz has anything to worry about here. Just for the hotel, Jacques Garcia, a decorator I normally like, coined a new style, High Tape-à-l'Oeil. One day I'm going to write a book: *When Bad Hotels Happen to Good Designers.* The Ritz will not get off so easy when Shangri-La and Mandarin Oriental open branches, in 2009 and 2010, respectively. Located off Place du Trocadéro and with 118 rooms—many facing the Seine, a huge selling point—the Shangri-La Palais d'Iena has pedigree: it was built by Napoleon's great-nephew, Prince Roland Bonaparte, in 1897. Didier Le Calvez

has been poached from the George V to manage the Palais d'Iena, and Rochon, surprise, is the decorator. The designs of the 150-room Mandarin on the Ritz client are implicit in its location: around the corner from Place Vendôme, in an Art Deco town house at 247 Rue St.-Honoré.

Every time the Ritz looks down, someone else is biting its heels. The Bristol bought the bank next door to create 27 new rooms, increasing its inventory by a full 16 percent. The Plaza Athénée is sending guests out into Paris empowered with a "private concierge": a GPS-equipped PDA loaded with an address book, cultural itineraries, and dictionaries. (A no-brainer, but then why didn't the Ritz think of it?) Others of the Plaza's attempts to distinguish itself are meaningless, unless you sleep with your security detail (the 5,382-square-foot Royal Suite is billed as the largest in the capital), or just plain silly ($35 "alco-mist" mojitos, served in spray bottles in the bar).

In the end the most serious threat to the Ritz may be the Crillon, which was purchased in late 2005 by Starwood Capital, the private real estate investment firm headed by Barry Sternlicht, the founder of Starwood Hotels & Resorts. The Crillon is poised to become a chain (a posh chain, anyway), with Paris as the flagship and projected outposts in London, Rome, and New York. To ensure that all the aesthetic cues it gives are the right ones, the

A gilded swan spout in a bathroom.

Dishes from the hotel's organic room-service menu.

Place de la Concorde landmark is undergoing a redesign this year.

The one old opponent the Ritz needs no longer bother about is the Meurice, which is a little late to the party in tapping Philippe Starck to remake its lobby and *jardin d'hiver*. Touchingly, executives say the point in bringing in Starck is to help the hotel stay up-to-date. It's a desperate move.

News of Starck's rendezvous with the Meurice (a lobby and *jardin d'hiver* cannot be called a marriage) broke the week I was at the Ritz, but did not even merit a mention in the War Room. I would be hopeless as a Ritz department head because to reach the room you have to pass before the office of the hotel's president, Frank Klein, something I could never do without a shiver. Klein is sentenced to be remembered as the senior Ritz official on whose watch Princess Diana and her boyfriend Dodi Fayed died following dinner at the hotel, in 1997. Given the wolfish mood of the paparazzi that night, many—including a lot of Diana freaks—think the couple should never have been allowed to leave the Ritz. Klein was on vacation, but that fact hasn't let him entirely off the hook. His position is especially ticklish because the hotel happens to be owned by Dodi's uncles and his father, Mohamed Al Fayed. The brothers also own Harrods, and when you phone the store there's a menu option that tells you what to dial "if your call has anything to do with Dodi or Diana." Al Fayed is still pursuing his theory, voiced in court, that the Duke of Edinburgh engineered to have the Princess of Wales and his son murdered. Whatever the truth, two things seem sure: Al Fayed will continue to be denied British citizenship. And the Queen and Philip will never sleep at the Ritz.

Whether or not Klein's presence would have prevented the tragedy, Al Fayed has stood by him. When his family acquired the Ritz in 1979, business

The Espadon team, with chef de cuisine Michel Roth (center).

Colin Field, tender of the hotel's
Hemingway Bar, in action.

was poor, the hotel in an advanced state of decay. It still had one of those old-fashioned plug-type switchboards, and people were staying away in droves. Al Fayed and Klein made a formidable team, giving the place buzz and bulldozing it into modern times. Al Fayed seems to understand that after himself (he is, after all, the check-writer), it is Klein who makes the hotel go.

"Are we still recording in room 256?" Acar asked one day, by way of opening the morning briefing.

Yes, construction noise from a neighboring building was being documented to support a legal case. Every time a certain level was reached, the Ritz's lawyer received an e-mail.

"Good," Acar said. "Call the bailiff today, and make sure guests checking out sign something saying they were disturbed by the noise. What about Sharon Stone?"

At the mention of the once-hot actress—who has taken to shilling beauty products for women of a certain age and who travels under the pretentious pseudonym Docteur Katrine Davis—everyone tried to pretend that *Basic Instinct 2* hadn't immediately gone south.

"She's coming in today," Acar announced. "Are we doing anything special for her? Does she have anything to do with the new Eastwood movie and the press conference he's giving here?"

"No, Stone is in Paris for Dior," someone volunteered. "We've got her in the Chanel Suite. She's arriving with her sister and friends, like always."

"Is Eastwood married?" Acar wondered.

"I know he was once, but he got div..."

"Give him a hard pillow. No, seriously. Today is Valentine's Day. We've got to do something that says Valentine's Day in Paris. Pink macaroons. But no candles. No open flames. Has anything been organized for the staff? Let's get a heart-shaped cake in the cafeteria."

Acar scanned a printout of the day's arrivals. "Bündchen—I don't see her here."

"No, that's next week, Fashion Week," offered the reservations manager. "Six nights."

"Okay, but the hotel is still too hot. Can we get the temperature turned down to twenty-two [72 degrees]? I'm dying."

Acar fielded a report from the food and beverage manager (a spoiled batch of Ritz-label champagne would have to be withdrawn) before tossing a hand grenade: Acar had just discovered that twin beds were being pushed together to create kings, and sold as such.

"I'm warning you guys, that's not the way we do business. You sell a king, you deliver a king. If there are none and it means losing three rooms, we lose three rooms. Nobody should pay eight hundred euros and get less than what they were sold. We're a brand. Aston Martin doesn't promise one thing and give another. Rate integrity comes with value. Have a nice day."

While Acar is right to insist on real kings, an uncommon if not unique policy, there is some sense that his energies could at times be more profitably spent—say, getting the concierges off autopilot. A request for an out-of-print book came back with a note saying it does not exist in French. In fact, the book *only* exists in French. Staying at the Park Hyatt, I gave out the same task, and a simple Google search landed a copy in seconds. Another day, I asked a Ritz concierge what Métro to take to the American Hospital. "I don't advise a Métro," the man said. "A taxi will be easier." Easier? Really? He wasn't joking.

As a hotel whose identity is embedded in details so fine, niceties so "minor," that many are felt rather than noticed, the Ritz deserves better. History does not record César Ritz's thoughts on tooth glasses, but the current practice of stowing them out of sight in medicine cabinets is pure him. Charles Ritz, César's son, held that the hotel's past was important only for maintaining "the indisputable traditions." An incomplete list would have to include the key-shaped light switches in bronze filigree, the bedside command boxes for summoning a waiter, the kitschy but irresistible gold swan fixtures from which water flows in the bathrooms, the pink bath towels, and the possibility of having your sheets laundered with *savon de Marseilles*. Also indelibly Ritz (but never, as Charles asserted, ritzy) are the balloon awnings over the entrance, the 361-foot-long gallery of 89 retail vitrines, L'Espadon's faux-branch armchairs and ceiling cloudscape, and the lobby that is not a lobby. (Ritz père thought that big conventional ones attracted loiterers.) And what could be more Ritz than the delivery of your dinner check, as the service handbook requires, 60 seconds after it is asked for... unless it's the quaint wooden carousel on which reception hangs your key?

There's a lot to love at the Ritz. But it's a mistake to try to monetize the experience, as natural and tempting as that is. It's impossible in any case to assign a value to the bewitchingly nostalgic act of turning a key-shaped light switch. A night at the Ritz is a priceless education. No voluptuary can afford to die dumb.

The Imperial Suite,
on the second floor.

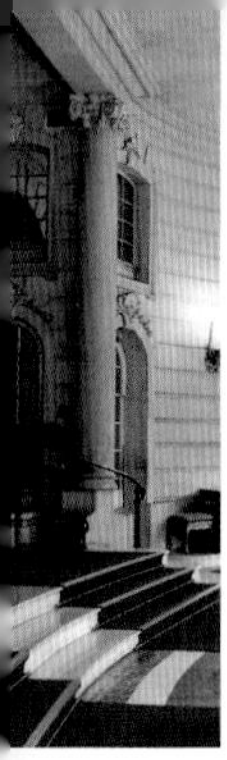

Travelers' Guide to Place Vendôme and Nearby

EXPLORING THE OPÉRA AND TUILERIES

Place Vendôme, home of the Paris Ritz, lies between the region around the Opéra to the north and the riverside Tuileries area to the south. The 19th-century grandeur of Baron Haussmann's *grands boulevards* offsets the bustle of the bankers, theatergoers, sightseers, and shoppers who frequent the Opéra quarter. The Tuileries includes the vast Place de la Concorde, the Jardins des Tuileries, and the Louvre. Close to the Place Vendôme, itself a heady mix of stores for the rich and the chic, are two of Paris's foremost shopping streets, Rue de Rivoli and Rue St.-Honoré.

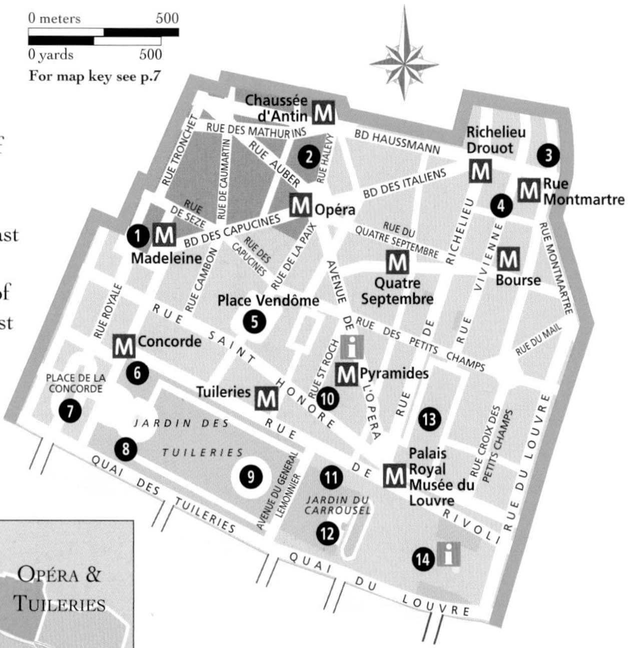
0 meters 500
0 yards 500
For map key see p.7
Chaussée d'Antin
Rue des Mathurins
Rue Tronchet
Rue de Caumartin
Rue Auber
Rue Halévy
Bd Haussmann
Richelieu Drouot
Rue Montmartre
Bd des Italiens
Opéra
Rue de Sèze
Bd des Capucines
Madeleine
Rue Cambon
Rue des Capucines
Rue de la Paix
Rue du Quatre Septembre
Quatre Septembre
Rue Richelieu
Rue Vivienne
Bourse
Rue Montmartre
Place Vendôme
Rue Royale
Rue Saint Honoré
Concorde
Avenue de l'Opéra
Rue des Petits Champs
Rue du Mail
Rue St Roch
Pyramides
Place de la Concorde
Tuileries
Jardin des Tuileries
Quai des Tuileries
Avenue du General Lemonnier
Rue de Rivoli
Palais Royal Musée du Louvre
Rue Croix des Petits Champs
Rue du Louvre
Jardin du Carrousel
Quai du Louvre

While at the Ritz...

Arc de Triomphe du Carousel 12
Galerie Nationale du Jeu de Paume 6
Grévin 3
Jardin des Tuileries 9
La Madeleine 1
Les Passages 4
Musée de l'Orangerie 8
Musée des Arts Décoratifs 11
Musée du Louvre 14
Opéra National de Paris Garnier 2
Palais Royal 13
Place de la Concorde 7
Place Vendôme 5
St.-Roch 10

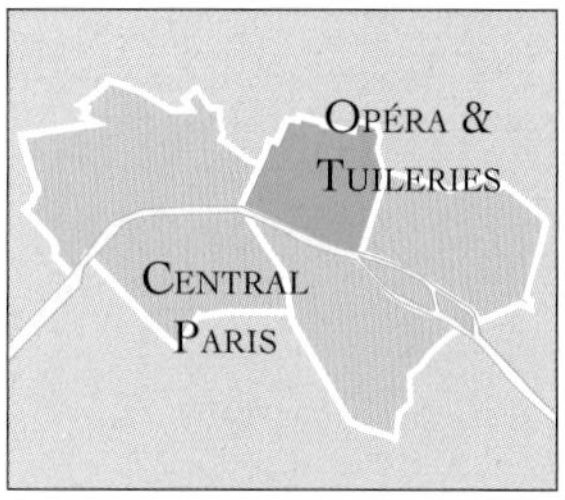
Opéra & Tuileries
Central Paris

WHERE TO STAY

Paris Ritz
15 Place Vendôme;
33-1/43-16-30-30;
ritzparis.com;
doubles from $$$$$.

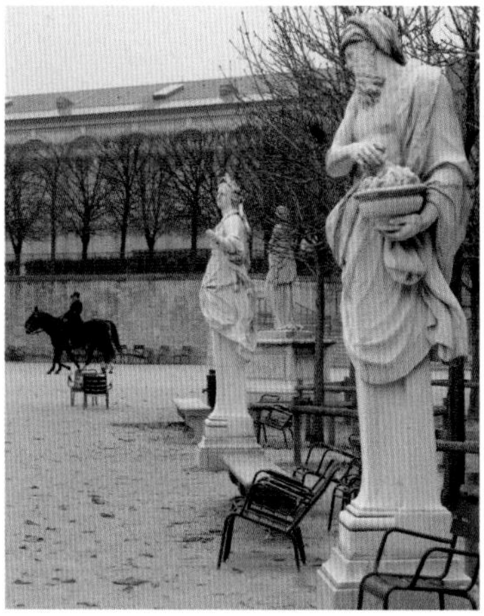

The Jardin des Tuileries.

TOP SIGHTS NEAR THE RITZ

Arc de Triomphe du Carousel 12
This rose-marble arch was built for Napoleon to celebrate his military victories, notably the Battle of Austerlitz in 1805.

Galerie Nationale du Jeu de Paume 6
The Jeu de Paume (literally "game of the palm") was built as two royal tennis courts by Napoleon III in 1851. It was later converted to hold French Impressionist art. The collection was moved to the Musée d'Orsay in 1986. The Jeu de Paume now exhibits contemporary art and houses the Centre Nationale de la Photographie.

Grévin 3
Historical scenes at this wax museum include Louis XIV at Versailles and the arrest of Louis XVI. Notable figures from the worlds of art, film, politics, and sport are also on display.

Jardin des Tuileries 9
These Neoclassical gardens once belonged to the Palais des Tuileries, which the Communards razed to the ground in 1871. The gardens were laid out in the 17th century by André Le Nôtre, who created the broad central avenue and topiary arranged in geometric designs. Le Nôtre's work can also be seen at the Château de Versailles.

La Madeleine 1
Modeled after a Greek temple, La Madeleine was begun in 1764 but not consecrated as a church until 1845. A Corinthian colonnade encircling the exterior supports a sculpted frieze. The lavishly decorated interior has domed ceilings and fine sculptures.

Les Passages 4
Paris's early-19th-century glass-roofed shopping arcades (known as *galeries* or *passages*) are concentrated between Boulevard Montmartre and Rue St.-Marc. One of the most charming is the Galerie Vivienne (off Rue des Petits Champs or Rue Vivienne), with its mosaic floor and excellent tearoom.

Musée de l'Orangerie ❽

The prime exhibits in this art gallery are eight of Monet's huge water lily canvases. The Walter-Guillaume collection covers works by Renoir, Picasso, Modigliani, and other modern masters from 1870 to 1900.

Musée des Arts Décoratifs ⓫

Occupying the northwest wing of the Louvre (along with the Musée de la Publicité and the Musée de la Mode et de la Textile), this museum offers an eclectic mix of decorative art and domestic design from the Middle Ages to the present day. (*See Living Rooms, pp.154–161.*)

Musée du Louvre ⓮

The world's largest museum unsurprisingly contains one of the world's most important collections of art and antiquities. To complete the superlatives, the building was once France's largest royal palace.

Opéra National de Paris Garnier ❷

This extravagant building, designed by Charles Garnier for Napoleon III in 1862, is famous for its Grand Staircase of white Carrara marble. The huge auditorium, bedecked in red and velvet, has a false ceiling painted by Chagall in 1964.

Arched entrance to Musée de l'Orangerie.

A view of the Place de La Concorde, with temple-like La Madeleine visible in the distance.

Palais Royal ⓭

A former royal palace, this building now houses the Councils of State and the Ministry of Culture. Built by Cardinal Richelieu in 1632, it passed to the crown on his death 10 years later, and was the childhood home of Louis XIV. The dukes of Orléans acquired it in the 18th century.

Place de la Concorde ❼

The magnificent square was designed in 1775 by Jacques-Ange Gabriel to display a statue of Louis XV. Less than 20 years later, during the French Revolution, the statue was replaced by the guillotine. The 3,200-year-old Luxor obelisk, two fountains, and eight statues personifying French cities were added in the 19th century.

Place Vendôme ❺

Perhaps the best example of 18th-century elegance in Paris, architect Jules Hardouin-Mansart's royal square was begun in 1698. Originally, the plan was to house academies and embassies behind its arcaded façades, but instead bankers moved in and built sumptuous mansions.

St.-Roch ❿

This huge church was designed by Jacques Lemercer, architect of the Louvre, and its foundation stone was laid by Louis XIV in 1653. A treasure trove of religious art, it also contains the tombs of royal gardner André Le Nôtre, philosopher Denis Diderot, and playwright Pierre Corneille.

SEE ALSO

For more on Paris:
Paris Modern pp.18–21
Coco Loco pp.190–191
For Versailles:
Biking Through Versailles pp.28–29
For the Musée du Louvre:
Living Rooms pp.162–163

Photographs by Matthew Hranek

New Wave Inns

FROM PROVENCE TO THE DORDOGNE, NEXT-GENERATION INNS ARE AWASH IN MODERNISM, MOROCCAN EXOTICISM, FLEMISH AUSTERITY—EVERYTHING BUT TRADITIONAL FRENCH COUNTRY STYLE. BY CHRISTOPHER PETKANAS

DORDOGNE

PROVENCE

There's a new wind blowing in France—or is that a storm kicking up? Guesthouses—*maisons d'hôtes*—are in a delirious state of revolution.

In the old model, the kids went off to university, their rooms (minus the Johnny Hallyday posters) were done up with a wing, a prayer, a staple gun, a bolt of Napoleonic toile de Jouy (purchased on a special trip to Paris at the Marché St.-Pierre discount fabric market), and that was that. Maybe the radiators worked, maybe they didn't. The towels were leftovers, thin and sandpapery. The croissants had freezer burn. If you were a chatelain, you accepted paying guests as a way of paying for repairs of the family tapestry (Brussels)—or, more urgently, the roof.

In a dramatic reversal, the contemporary model is conceived—designed—as a *maison d'hôte*; clumsy retrofitting is finished. And because owners are serious about getting a return on their investment, their MO is more professional. The best of these *maisons d'hôtes* are also tiny, with as few as two guest rooms: You feel like you own the place.

But perhaps nothing has changed so much as the look, which has progressed from quaint and nostalgic to exotic and transporting. The map says Provence, but one *maison d'hôte* can't seem to make up its mind if it's in Morocco, India, or New Mexico.

The pool at Moroccan-inspired L'Ange et L'Éléphant, a new inn in Provence.

Moroccan doors framing the entrance to L'Ange et L'Éléphant, just off Maussane's main square.

Mont Ste.-Victoire is the unlikely site of an Asian fantasy, lit with *washi*-paper Noguchi lanterns. In the Dordogne, a vernacular farmhouse goes head-to-head with two lean-and-mean, 21st-century pavilions. Furnished with modern classics by Le Corbusier and Mies van der Rohe, a medieval castle lifts its defensive bulk above the Ardèche River.

Luxurious double-faced wool-and-alpaca throws, L'Occitane amenities, and Olivier Desforges bath sheets will have you pinching yourself. Have *maisons d'hôtes* really come to this? They have. No, Fifi, we're not in Clermont-Ferrand anymore.

L'ANGE ET L'ÉLÉPHANT, MAUSSANE-LES-ALPILLES, PROVENCE

"Let's get this party started!"

This being France, what the person at the next table actually said to me was, *"Allez les enfants, la fête commence main-te-NANT!"*

Historically, provincial *maisons d'hôtes* are a lot of things—deliciously louche, impossibly cute, poignantly decrepit—but rarely are they scene-y.

L'Ange et L'Éléphant is the almost freakish, salutary exception, an all-in-one inn, restaurant, café, tea salon, and boutique. You might also call it a hangout, one that answers the ancient national need to be *depaysé*, or lifted away, by a mood, an atmosphere, an ambience—but without having to get on a plane.

Provence, as everyone knows, is the country's most hedonistic region, but no one does pleasure-seeking—which, to be frank, often means squeaking by with doing as little as possible—like this pocket of the Bouches-du-Rhône. You smoke yourself to death over a pastis, toss a steel ball in an umpteenth game of *boules*, take three hours to do the marketing for lunch, read and reread the sports page of *Le Provençal*—and before you know it, it's time for a nap. Idleness isn't just its own reward here in the heart of Frédéric Mistral country, but a virtue. L'Ange et L'Éléphant taps into this lifestyle in a rather edgy way. It's a huge success, the frustrated envy of every Maussane shopkeeper and hotel and restaurant proprietor intent on relieving tourists of their euros.

L'Ange et L'Éléphant requisitions a massive 18th-century staging post. It's a lovely three-minute walk from the town's main square, down an allée of plane trees and past the handsome washhouse inaugurated by Napoleon III in 1865 and the butcher selling garrigue-grazed Maussane lamb under a registered trademark. St.-Rémy is just on the other side of the Alpilles mountains. Les Baux, with its spectacular

84

The romantic mezzanine suite at L'Ange et L'Éléphant.

wind-hollowed bauxite cliffs, lurks above. Like St.-Rémy, Maussane suffers from being fashionable, but unlike the former it still retains a degree of authenticity. Despite the hype engulfing Provence, despite the bad food and subdivisions and *grandes surfaces* (ghastly stadium-sized supermarkets that, to be fair, are also filled with guilty pleasures), Maussane still resembles the sort of agrarian stronghold rich in folkways eulogized by Mistral in his memoirs. I rented a house here 20 years ago and amazingly, nothing much has changed since, except that during the summer *fête votive* (the feast day of the patron saint of the village church and the village itself), the girls who perform in the magnificently cheesy revue have harder bodies and are showing more of them.

What makes L'Ange et L'Éléphant so special? As the vise screws of *"l'esprit boho"* take another quarter-turn on the French imagination, it's a relief to see that *l'esprit* hasn't been totally co-opted by Parisians striking a subversive pose. This is the real thing. The fact that L'Ange et L'Éléphant is a little destabilizing and hard to nail down only heightens the experience. It's a cultural and decorative stew. There were moments when I felt like I was in Tangier—or was it Chandernagore? Scratch that. What it really feels like (I think) is Santa Fe.

On motorcycles and in BMW's they come to sip melon wine, nibble chicken in coconut milk (amateurish and eccentric, the food is far from the point), and nuzzle their dates under the stars in a sprawling courtyard. It's appointed not with all that boilerplate stuff that romanticizes French rural life but with tole cacti, daybeds from Afghanistan lashed with buffalo thongs, embroidered straw rugs ravaged by the sun and rain, cedar panels of lacy moucharaby, old beaten shutters—and vintage Coca-Cola picnic coolers. (Nearly all of the above is for sale, augmented by Fez pottery, horn cups, and sequined babouches in the boutique.) A giant blow-up chair skims the surface of the kind of featureless anti–swimming-pool swimming pool the French term a *bassin*. It's all casually banged together, the service is beyond relaxed, but it works.

The party goes on all night to an insinuating sound track of the African chanteuse Judith Sephuma and Brazil's Rosalia de Souza, the neighbors—some of them farmers who must be up with the sun—be damned. (Even guests cruelly deprived of sleep by the music, nattering, and

clinking of glasses sometimes feel that Juliette Godeau Ledieu and Joël Gourlot, L'Ange et L'Éléphant's owners, go too far in the pursuit of a good time.) Down the lane, workers at Moulin Jean-Marie Cornille, the most famous olive-oil mill in France, have been at it for many hours before the couple have even thought about raising the shades.

It's difficult to imagine, but Godeau Ledieu and Gourlot are veterans of the pharmaceutical industry. They are the only *aubergiste*s in France (possibly in the world) ever to have met in a Johnson & Johnson laboratory.

"It's that feeling of being somewhere else, yet perfectly at home," says Gourlot of the cloistered mini-universe he and Godeau Ledieu summoned from scratch. "L'Ange et L'Éléphant is an anachronism. Some people put their nose through the gate and walk away, so there's an auto-selection process that actually suits us. In this way the only people here are people who want to be here. We're not for everyone."

That is just as well, as there are only two guest rooms. One is perfectly sweet, though it gives directly onto the pool and is not much bigger than a cocktail napkin. The shower stall, open on one side, is so near the bed you are always afraid of turning on the water for fear of soaking the taffeta curtain

The Hirondelle room at Le Canard à Trois Pattes, in Tamniès.

*One of several alfresco dining spots at
Le Canard a Trois Pattes.*

(*folo*) that drapes it. Nothing sums up Godeau Ledieu's improvised style like the bedcover, unless it's the hand towels, which someone has very patiently edged with little silk knots that look just like my Charvet cuff links.

Reached via a private, exterior corkscrew staircase from India in elaborately worked iron, the 750-square-foot suite has two bedrooms (one on a mezzanine), a salon that drifts into an open kitchen, and a vast terrace that keeps an eye on all the goings-on in the courtyard below. The chef d'oeuvre here is the bathroom's waist-high unglazed terra-cotta jar from Rajasthan cradling a sink from Morocco in *maillechort*, a copper, zinc, and nickel alloy. My bed had an acid-dipped metal headboard in the shape of an ogee arch. Taking up the book on the nightstand before going to sleep, I saw that the previous guest had gotten to page 229 of *Le Tour du Monde en 80 Jours*.

LE CANARD A TROIS PATTES, TAMNIÈS, DORDOGNE

Flush with medieval and Renaissance monuments, Sarlat is the tourism capital of the Dordogne, and everything you have heard about it is true. The only language spoken is English, iterated with an English accent. Every perpetrator has a camper, a baby stroller, and at least one dog, and in summer they make Saturday, market day, a misery.

The antidote lies in a hamlet 7½ miles to the north, at a gently perched 15th-century farmhouse with five guest rooms and an arcadian view of soft hills flecked with cows as big as medium-size rental cars. No one is more aware than I am that this is exactly the kind of vignette country people make fun of city people for even registering, but I'm going to describe it anyway: The cows pass in front of the house twice a day, on their way to and from being pastured. A farmer leads the herd (though herd is much too big a word for his troop of four or five), putting up as he goes a string barrier to keep the animals from devastating the neighbors' grass. His son brings up the rear, taking the string down as quickly as it went up. All this takes place under your nose, while you look out of your bedroom window.

If that scene doesn't have you reaching for the Internet to make a reservation at Le Canard a Trois Pattes, this may: the principal structure is an exceptional example of colloquial *perigourdin* architecture, with a façade of limestone blocks in a deep, drenched-ocher color; schist roof shingles; and knobbly pisé floors—schist chiseled into small, triangular stones driven pointy-side-down into wet, beaten earth. Framing the house, and staging a prickly confrontation with it, are two blunt cubic pavilions with flat roofs built on the footprints of a

Le Canard a Trois Pattes's house-made fig tart.

*A view of the pool, guesthouse, and
annex at Le Canard a Trois Pattes.* 87

Château de Balazuc, restored in 2006, in Balazuc.

The modern-classic salon at Château de Balazuc.

pigpen and a bread house. Studio Carré Rouge and La Habanna, which sleeps five and has a small hardworking kitchen, are not totally disinterested in tradition, however: their wide pine siding makes reference to the region's tobacco-drying sheds.

Armand Van Lierde and Greet Decreus, Belgian architects who had their own practice in Antwerp before coming to the Dordogne, are the B&B owners from heaven: discreet, cultivated, laissez-faire. Decreus is also a decorative painter, Van Lierde an artist. In the dining room, where chairs of rigid polyurethane foam by Maarten Van Severen for Vitra are pulled up to an old refectory table, one of Van Lierde's works leans against a wall, a huge red field with a heart lying on its side, perhaps recovering from a wound. And in an area where they would find a way to turn foie gras into ice cream if they thought anybody would eat it, the dishes Decreus coaxes out of her plump, retro Smeg fridge and butter-yellow Aga are models of freshness, sanity, and simplicity: grilled eggplant *involtini* piped with goat cheese, cherry-tomato risotto, cinnamony apple tart. Seafood arrives right at the gate via an ambulant fishmonger who receives regular deliveries from the Atlantic.

In the atelier, in the kitchen, Decreus and Van Lierde demonstrate great reductionist style. They subscribe to *wabi-sabi,* the Japanese aesthetic system that finds beauty in imperfection, chance, decay, impermanence, natural wear and tear, and making something from nothing. Van Lierde gives two examples: "We had some not especially pretty stones left over from restoring the house and made a pile of them in a spot that happens to be favorable for raspberries and blackberries," he says. "Now the bushes are growing among and around the stones, creating a happy, artful composition. A section of the pisé floor in the salon has sunken in, and some of the stones have come loose, but I find it very beautiful. I won't touch it."

Swallow, the only accommodation in the main building, is named for the bird's nest tacked to a ceiling beam, another instance of *wabi-sabi.* Floating the mattress in the middle of the room, with no headboard, no nightstand, no bedside lamp, no nothing is a provocation I understand but reject as impractical and even a little sadistic: sleeping here, or trying to, I felt totally unmoored. The only other furnishings are a butterfly chair, a folding park chair in flaking paint, and a huge ottoman in hairy chocolate cowhide. Separated from the bedroom by

a half-wall clad in chestnut planks, the bathroom has a sumptuous slipper tub that was found languishing in a field and re-porcelained.

Château des Milandes and Manoir d'Eyrignac are so close by I could not find a reason not to visit them. Milandes is where Josephine Baker raised all those adopted children and where the original of her legendary banana skirt is exhibited. Eyrignac's grounds follow an 18th-century Italianate design and are known to garden enthusiasts around the world. Revenge on the campers and baby strollers was not my object in stopping in Sarlat on the way back, but what a bonus. After taking a lazy look around St. Sacerdos's cathedral, the bishop's palace, and the courthouse and filling my basket with a tin of foie gras and a liter of walnut oil, I raced home to the arms of the Duck with Three Feet.

CHÂTEAU DE BALAZUC, BALAZUC, ARDÈCHE

After the Revolution, property belonging to emigrés was confiscated by the state and auctioned "*à la bougie*"—with a candle. According to this picturesque custom, the winning bidder was whoever made the last offer before the candle burned out.

But what if you staged an auction and nobody came? That was the fate of two 1792 sales that tried

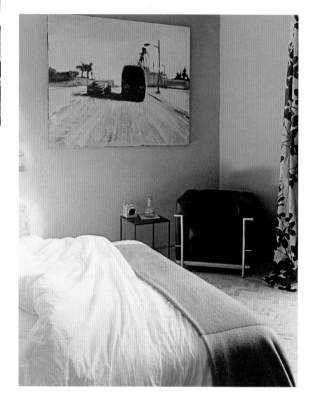

to unload the 11th-century Château de Balazuc, whose host bourg (full-time population: 335) is located in the lower Ardèche on a bluff high above the temperamental Ardèche River, 63 miles north of Avignon. It's a gray (all that Jurassic limestone), isolated, fantastically lonely place of vaulted passageways, houses that seem to grow out of the cliff face, and vacationing canoeists whose hands the locals like to bite. The villain in a long history of poverty and suffering is what Yale professor John Merriman names in his *Stones of Balzac* the "'ungrateful' soil."

The auctions took place while the count who owned the castle was licking his wounds and basically just trying to stay alive in England. There was a lot of melted wax. Eventually, almost grudgingly, a farmer stepped up to buy the château before yet another candle spent itself and a cheerless thread of smoke filled the sale room. He paid a derisory 625 livres and used the castle, Gothic fireplace and all, as a rather grandiose outbuilding (even the andirons have survived, gorgeously intact). Combined with its awful condition, disaffection for the château ran so high that it brought more than 24,000 livres less than the village gristmill, which had the advantage of being revenue-producing, and only 175 livres more than the humble communal bread oven. What all this illustrates is that square footage is a contemporary

obsession. A castle with a river view, even one in bad shape, at fire-sale prices—no one today could say no.

The last time the château changed hands, in 2002, it was still being abused in the same depressing fashion, this time by a grower of wine grapes. In one of those big, brave, life-changing moves that have a way of yielding a great guest experience, Virginie and Daniel Boulenger ditched their careers as auto-parts engineers (well, somebody has to do that job) to open a four-room *maison d'hôte*, erase the inglorious chapters in the castle's past, and restore its seigneurial dignity.

They accomplished this in ways that would not have occurred to your old-school fixer-upper of fortresslike medieval châteaux. Three of the guest rooms are situated off the salon, where a muscle-bound steel-and-glass staircase and bridge lead to the Boulengers' private apartments. Furniture runs to Le Corbusier club chairs and Barcelona chairs in audacious white leather, designs whose flashing metal frames look wonderful against the matte slate and brick herringbone of the floors. Even more tonic and startling is the collection of modern art, including one painting in Jean-Marc Dallanegra's pressure-cooker series and a portrait by Troy Henriksen that pays homage to Jean-Michel

A colorful breakfast setting at Château de Balazuc.

The best of these maisons d'hôtes *are tiny,
with as few as two guest rooms: You feel like
you own the place*

*Lunch on the terrace at
Château de Balazuc.*

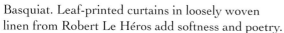

Basquiat. Leaf-printed curtains in loosely woven linen from Robert Le Héros add softness and poetry.

Dinner is served at one seating on a terrace overlooking the river under a canopy of Virginia creeper amid ad-libbed bouquets of dried grasses, wild fennel, and thistles. Daniel takes great care with the seating plan, and plates are scrupulously changed between courses, just as at a real dinner party. However good Virginie was at designing dashboards and rearview mirrors, she could not have been better at it than she is at cooking. A typical meal might begin with a cheeky "tarte Tatin" of eggplant with sun-dried tomatoes and pine nuts, then move on to a *gigot de sept heures* (leg of lamb cooked in a slow oven for seven hours, until it can be carved with a spoon), wheat berries, and buttered string beans from a neighbor's garden. Roasted figs with cardamom is a popular dessert. No one turns in without a mug of house tisane, lemon verbena and star anise or linden blossom and mint.

A meal across the bridge at Le Viel Audon, 20 minutes on foot from the château, is just as satisfying, but in an utterly rustic way you would have thought lost. The hamlet is a species of cooperative where if you're older than 6 and younger than 26 you can go to learn bread-baking, beekeeping, animal husbandry, and more. Lunch is a board piled with thick shards of ham, dried sausage, cornichons, and goat cheeses in three stages of maturity. And it wouldn't be the Ardèche if there wasn't *caillette*, a mixture of Swiss chard leaves, pork, and pig's liver wrapped in caul fat. Just in case you haven't had enough cheese, it appears again at dessert, freshly strained and molded, topped with chestnut cream or blackberry-and-blueberry jam.

Balazuc's vegetation is Mediterranean. But as the village is only 10 miles south of "the olive line," the cutoff point for the cultivation of olive trees, no one should go expecting Provence. Balazuc has none of that region's easy talent for voluptuousness. Pleasure has never been its own reward here, though the Boulengers are having great success swimming against time and history.

LA QUINTA DES BAMBOUS, ST.-MARC-JAUMEGARDE, PROVENCE

As little as 10 years ago, La Quinta des Bambous would have opened, sputtered, and died. People weren't ready for an Asian-inspired *maison d'hôte* in France, however beautiful, especially not one with a view of Mont Ste.-Victoire. Then, a guesthouse in the shadow of the mountain that so preoccupied Cézanne would have practically guaranteed a "Provençal experience," meaning the quilts, the prints, the lavender, the sweet breakfast *fougasse*, the chipped checked-tinplate salt canister on the kitchen windowsill.

But a Japanese rock garden would have been seen as not just alien but heretical. Not to mention headboards fashioned out of tatami mats, Javanese colonial furniture, and cement floors with ideograms for happiness spelled out in river stones.

What a difference a decade makes. In a new, less nostalgic and sentimental climate that goes beyond pastis and pottery, and that finally has travelers relaxing their quaint and hoary expectations, reservations at La Quinta are rarer than hen's teeth; to snag one during the summer music festival in neighboring Aix you had better know the mayor or someone similarly placed, or change your plans and go to Brittany. The only thing that stands between the *maison d'hôte* and Aix is a lovely 10-minute drive in the same hallowed countryside as Château de Vauvenargues, where Picasso lived his last years and is buried. La Quinta is sited on the edge of an immense forest of pines and live oaks, the starting point of romantic trails that lead to two dams: Bimont, which supplies Aix and Marseilles, and Zola, which was built by the novelist's engineer father, François, in 1854. There are other houses nearby, but the vegetation and spacing are such that as a guest you are only vaguely aware of them; privacy is not compromised.

A single story of smooth whitewashed stucco erected around a courtyard paved with loose stones, La Quinta hews freely (very freely) to a traditional Chinese plan, with each wing serving a precise, dedicated function such as eating, receiving, and sleeping. A roof of glazed and unglazed canal tiles lifts ever so discreetly at the corners, a nod to pagodas but also, just to confuse things, to the quintas around Lisbon, where owners Anne and Philippe Berthier lived after she folded her wings as an Air France stewardess and while he was a senior executive at IBM. Covered terraces projecting from either end of the building look like teahouses, if you squint. They flank an exquisitely plain 41-by-11-foot pool that owes its twinkle to flecks of mica in the anthracite finish. The pool terminates in a flat teak bridge and, just beyond it, a contiguous pond of koi, lotuses, and water lilies Anne brought back from Vietnam. Secreted in that sentence is everything you need to know about why La Quinta looks the way it does: Anne is French-Vietnamese. (Philippe is 100 percent French.) The *maison d'hôte* is a lab for exploring the visual aspects of her cultural heritage.

Of the three smallish guest rooms, two share the same access as the Berthiers' wing and have courtyard terraces (they aren't especially close, but in Jasmin I could hear someone blow his nose in Lotus). Pivoine is much more independent, with a private entrance and an outdoor sitting area that opens onto the forest and offers a heart-catching glimpse of Ste.-Victoire. The rooms are pleasant enough, with kitchenettes behind shoji-style screens, but they're not going to change the world. Haven't we all moved on from the basin sink? And, er, fiberglass tubs? The food, limited to breakfast, also needs rethinking. A tiered and lacquered Chinese wedding basket left on guests' dining tables the night before is a nice way around forcing them to commit to a breakfast time before they've even put on their pajamas, but there are obvious limitations, starting with the fact that nothing is hot. The most thrilling thing in my caddy was a slice of banana bread, if you don't count the foil-wrapped butter pats. *Très* zen.

Anne's minimalist impulses are much more digestible when she's celebrating the ancient Japanese art of rock placement. Interspersed with bamboo, the boulders in her garden are metaphors for islands; gravel, for the sea. (La Quinta's wind chimes are not a metaphor for anything, except maybe annoyance; when no one was looking I disabled them.) In the days when samurai were still a menace, the moodiest rocks with the biggest personalities were sometimes acquired by force. Anne avoids drawing her sword when someone has a stone she wants, though she does have the name of a good wholesaler outside Yokohama.

A curious local near Le Canard a Trois Pattes, in the Dordogne.

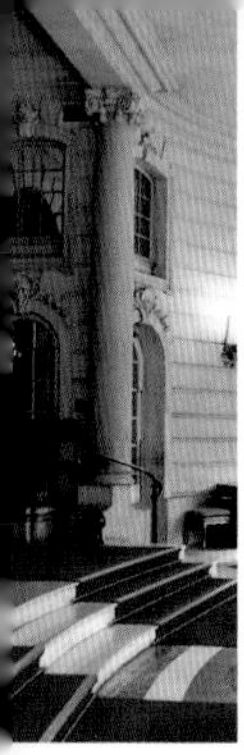

Travelers' Guide to Southern French Inns

WHEN TO GO
May and June are pleasant and warm; avoid July and August, when the Dordogne, the Ardèche, and Provence are at their busiest. September is crisp and clear across much of France, and temperatures stay in the 60's.

GETTING THERE
Air France (airfrance.com) offers daily flights from Paris to Marseilles, Avignon, and Bordeaux for under $200, or opt for France's high-speed TGV train (tgv.co.uk). The distances between L'Ange et L'Éléphant, Château de Balazuc, and La Quinta des Bambous are easily covered by car, and together they make a nice circuit.

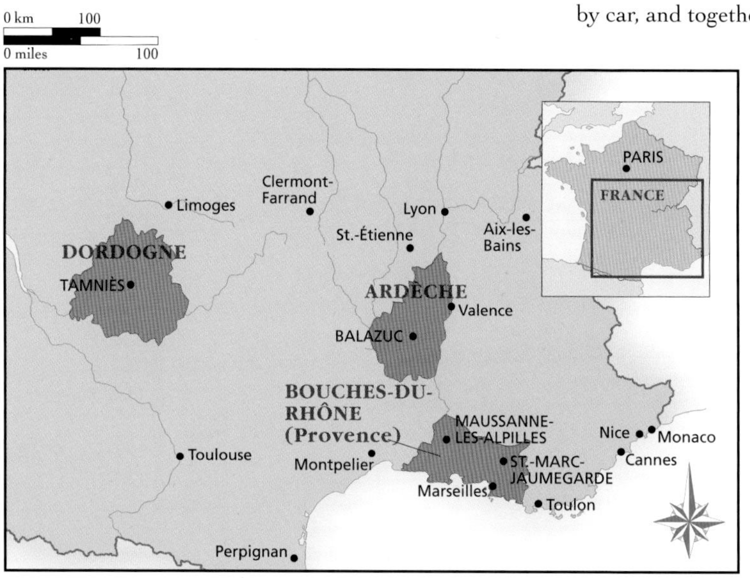

WHERE TO STAY
L'Ange et L'Éléphant
9 Rue de la Reine Jeanne,
Mausanne-les-Alpilles, Provence;
33-4/90-54-18-34;
doubles from $$.

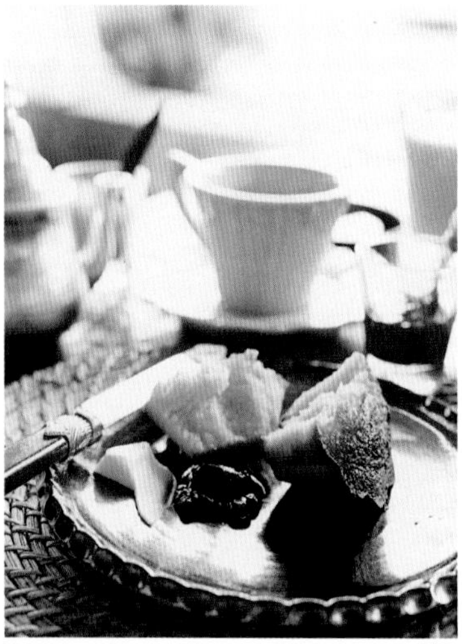

Breakfast of lemon cake and espresso at L'Ange et L'Éléphant, in Provence.

Le Canard à Trois Pattes
Le Castanet, Tamniès, Dordogne;
33-5/53-59-13-85;
troispattes.com;
doubles from $$.

Château de Balazuc
Balazuc, Ardèche;
33-4/75-88-52-67;
chateaudebalazuc.com;
doubles from $$.

La Quinta des Bambous
Chemin des Ribas, St.-Marc-Jaumegarde, Provence;
33-4/42-24-91-62;
laquintadesbambous.free.fr;
doubles from $$.

WHERE TO EAT
Le Viel Audon
This rustic inn-cum-cooperative has a café on the premises that's open to visitors.
Balazuc, Ardèche;
33-4/75-37-73-80;
lunch for two $$.

WHAT TO DO
ARDÈCHE
Château de Balazuc
Rent a kayak or a canoe and ride the river below the property.
Le Fazo;
33-4/75-88-52-67;
balazuc-canoe.com;
canoe rentals from $50 per day,
kayak rentals from $28 per day.

DORDOGNE
Château des Milandes
Tour the historic castle once owned by music-hall star Josephine Baker. Part of the tour is devoted to her life.
Castelnaud-La-Chapelle;
33-5/53-59-31-21;
chateaudesmilandes.com.

Les Jardins du Manoir d'Eyrignac
Ten acres of hedges and greenery vigorously maintained by traditional French gardening techniques.
Salignac;
33-5/53-28-99-71;
eyrignac.com.

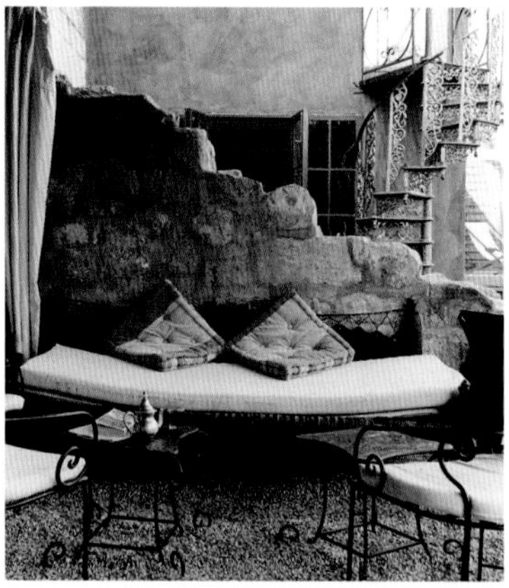

Eleventh-century charm at Château de Balazuc, in the Ardèche.

Fountains in the gardens of the Manoir d'Eyrignac, in the Dordogne.

SEE ALSO
For more on the Dordogne:
Back to the Land pp.140–143
For more on Provence:
On the Wagon pp.66–67
Bistros of Provence pp.114–115
Ma Vie en Rosé pp.150–151

WHAT TO READ
The Stones of Balazuc
By John Merriman.
Catalogs the history of the resilient
Ardèche River town.

Mes Origines, Mémoires et Récits
By Frédéric Mistral.
Recounts Mistral's childhood and
young adulthood, and has been
translated into English.

PROVENCE
Musée Frédéric Mistral
*The Nobel Prize–winning poet's residence
in Maillane houses his personal collection
of books and photographs.*
11 Ave. Lamartine, Maillane;
33-4/90-95-74-06.

Arles markets
*Provençal markets are always a treat, but
the Wednesday and Saturday morning
markets in Arles, located on Boulevard*

*Émile Combes and Boulevard des Lices,
are the best in the region.*

Atelier Cézanne
*Set among the landscapes he once
painted, Cézanne's Ste.-Victoire studio
is open by appointment to visitors daily,
from 10 a.m. to 5 p.m.*
9 Ave. Paul Cézanne,
Aix-en-Provence;
33-4/42-21-06-53;
atelier-cezanne.com.

INSIDER TIP
Consider planning your route
through the province of Drôme,
just east of the Ardèche. It's known
for its olives and *appellation d'origine
controlée* olive oil.

*Cézanne's studio, at
Aix-en-Provence.*

The Provençal hill town of Gordes,
an idyllic area for a rental.

Photographs by Marie Hennechart

Chez You

TRAVELERS RENTING A HOUSE IN THE FRENCH COUNTRYSIDE GAIN THE UNFORGETTABLE EXPERIENCE OF LIVING LIKE A NATIVE. HERE, A GUIDE TO FINDING A HOME AWAY FROM HOME. BY LESLIE BRENNER

• SARLAT

Living in the United States, but being married to a Frenchman, I had often dreamed of taking my family to live in France, even if just for a week or two. I pictured my son wearing a blue-and-white–striped shirt, curled up on a window seat reading Tintin in our Provençal *mas* (a stone farmhouse typical of the region) surrounded by lavender fields. Or our cottage in the Dordogne. Or our terra-cotta–roofed château in the Loire. Okay, maybe not a château, but why not the little guesthouse next to the château?

As it happens, a French-country fantasy, like many a dream these days, has a good chance of being fulfilled via some Internet research. We wanted a house for a week in April, large enough for eight: my husband, Thierry, and I; our son, Wylie; Thierry's parents, who live near Bordeaux; and Thierry's brother and his two kids. Almost immediately it became clear that French rental options were so widely available online that researching them could take over my life. So I decided to go with an established agency, many

The author's son, Wylie, on the bridge near Sarlat.

of which had Web sites that made it easy to narrow my choices by plugging in the region, the number of people, the amenities I wanted (pool, garden, dishwasher), and my price range. The choices that then appeared often offered a virtual tour, both of the exterior of the house and of all its rooms. And most added up to a per-day cost far less than a hotel would cost us, especially for a group of our size.

Peter Mayle's tales aside, many Americans looking to vacation in France choose to rent in the south because the weather is practically guaranteed to be good. We decided to look in the south-central region of the country, in the Dordogne, settling on the area around Les Eyzies-de-Tayac (a village with a wealth of caves, grottoes, and prehistoric art) and Sarlat (the largest town, home to a famous twice-weekly market in a medieval square). We had weighed whether to choose a village residence—which would offer a window into French life, since we could walk to the boulangerie and the café—or a country house, which would be even quieter and give our young son plenty of room to run.

On a Web site called holiday-rentals.com, I fell in love with a farmhouse 10 minutes outside of

Les Eyzies, and paid in full—$1,050, including a 2 percent surcharge for using a credit card. (Many companies don't take credit cards, but I wanted to use mine for added protection, having learned from my friend Susan Jamison, who'd recently spent a week with her family in Provence, that refunds are hard to come by.) Aside from my insisting on a credit card payment, the transaction seemed fairly typical—this site, like most I'd visited, required payment in full, plus a security deposit, eight weeks prior to departure.

Then, a week before we were to leave, the agency e-mailed to say the house wasn't available after all. Instead, I was being "rewarded" with a "more expensive" place well out of our target location. In a snit, I requested, and received, a full refund. But now we had plane tickets and no place to stay. I knew that Susan had had luck with rentvillas.com, a California-based agency, landing a four-bedroom *mas*—with a pool and within walking distance of the medieval hill town of Gordes—for $2,140 for a week. So I begged them to find me a desirable spot fast. Three days before we were supposed to head to the airport, we signed up for a four-bedroom house near Sarlat for $1,400.

We drove into La Roque–Gageac, a village built into a cliff along the Dordogne River, picked up

The façade of the author's rental house.

As it happens, a French-country fantasy, like many a dream these days, has a good chance of being fulfilled via some Internet research

Eating breakfast at home in the Dordogne.

Leslie Brenner on a village walk.

Dining at La Meynardie, in Salignac.

As the week passed—all too quickly—we each had experiences that became our own personal favorites. I frequented the *marché* at Sarlat, where I picked up amazing strawberries, white asparagus, and fresh goat cheese, among other things. But my best memory came after exploring Domme, a medieval *bastide*, when we had an extravagant picnic dinner on our terrace. The kids enjoyed the grottoes; riding the steam train along a truffle route; and, most of all, Château de Castelnaud, a 13th-century castle with a museum of medieval military history. And we all agreed that our favorite day was when we cruised the Dordogne in a traditional river barge, then had dinner at La Meynardie, a farmhouse-restaurant set in the middle of vineyards. Even everyday activities seemed special in these beautiful, unfamiliar surroundings. I'd buy bread and croissants at a bakery; shop for cheese, fruit, vegetables, and cured meat at the outdoor markets; and pick up everything else, including wine, at the supermarket. It all felt like a charmed experience, not a chore.

I'm willing to bet a year's vacation fund that this trip won't end up being the last days of chez nous.

keys at the *bar-tabac*, and climbed a steep path to the house. Wow. Our 700-year-old stone rental was much prettier than the photos we'd seen. It had a living room with a big fireplace, a terrace, and, in the kitchen, a farm table with a bottle of Cahors wine and a round loaf of bread to go with the platter of cheese in the fridge. These were homey touches; but they weren't the only reason that our rented house, and the town that surrounded it, came to feel like home. There were also the all-important fields of sunflowers, great french fries, and neighbors who disproved all those nasty French stereotypes, especially when Wylie attempted to speak their language. At home we were able to spread out, raise a rumpus, and raid a kitchen stocked with village market fare and enough croissants to keep everybody content. No one had to share a room. Of course, the kids—and even the grown-ups—found the odd thing to complain about, such as the Gallic idea of a shower (kind of like squirting yourself with a hose). But overall, we ended up loving our idyll in France.

The author and her family en route to Château de Castelnaud.

Travelers' Guide to Renting a House in France

WHERE TO RENT

Rental properties are available throughout France, from the rugged Atlantic coast and Haute-Savoie's Alpine slopes to the gastronomic paradise of the Dordogne, the wine-tasting heaven that is Languedoc-Roussillon, and the ever-popular Provence. Whatever your desired destination, with a little research you should be able to find a property that's just right for you.

RENTAL AGENCIES

Rentvillas.com

This group, which also specializes in Italy, handles about 244 houses in France, most of them in Provence. Customer service is a priority; a "travel adviser" rather than an agent will assist you. Rentvillas.com rates its properties on a scale of one to five stars, based on quality of the view, garden, rooms, and noise level. Clients' comments are posted uncensored on the Web site. Babysitters, maid service, and chefs are available at many properties—for a price. Credit cards are accepted.
800/726-6702 or 805/641-1650;
rentvillas.com;
cottages for four average $2,000 a week in low season, $3,000 in high; villas for seven (with pool) in high season from $3,836.

Ville et Village

With some 650 properties all over France and the able guidance of its owner, Carolyn Grote, this Berkeley, California-based agency is ideal if you're not sure which region is for you. Grote knows them all. She even has houses on Île de Ré, where it's notoriously hard for outsiders to get a foot in the door. Properties rented directly from owners are only available online, but a printed catalogue is available for all other rentals. One drawback: no credit cards.
510/559-8080;
villeetvillage.com;
cottages for four from $700 a week in low season, $920 in high; villas for six (with pool) from $3,700 high season.

Homes Away

For those in need of coddling and willing to pay for it (with a credit card), this Toronto-based firm represents 35 top-of-the-line French villas, some with chefs and all with a three-day-a-week cleaning service and the advice of an English-speaking host for 15 hours a week. The latter will not only stock the fridge and lay out a welcome buffet, but can also organize bike trips, hot-air balloon rides, even fireworks displays on request. You can also expect swimming pools, terraces, and superb views.
800/374-6637 or 416/920-1873;
homesaway.com;
three-bedroom houses from $7,000 a week in low season, $10,500 in high.

The market in Sarlat's Place de la Liberté, in the Dordogne, close to the house rented by author Leslie Brenner.

FINDING A GÎTE

Gîtes de France

This French government agency oversees a nationwide system of rural house and cottage rentals. Gîte means shelter in French, and these dwellings span the range of comfort levels, from single rooms in farmhouses to well-appointed estates. They're rated on a scale of one to five épis *(ears of corn). The good news: you can snag a great place for $600 per week in summer, and for considerably less if you're open to undiscovered locales. To find a property, explore the agency's Web site by region. Or request a catalogue for a particular area.* 33-1/49-70-75-75; gites-de-france.com.

Brittany Ferries

This British company produces a free compendium of Gîtes de France properties, with descriptions in English. 44-8705/561-600; brittany-ferries.com.

Not all *gîtes* belong to the official network. Find them on **gite.com** or by doing a Web search by town or region. One such *gîte* to check out: Aux Deux Soeurs, near St.-Rémy-de-Provence (**auxdeuxsoeurs-provence.com**), on the grounds of a 19th-century *bastide*, with a pool, baby-sitters, and English owners.

DIRECT LEASING

To find people who rent out houses, do a Web search by region, or try a global rental site such as **choice1. com**, **cyberrentals.com**, or **vrbo. com**, all of which allow you to specify what you're after and where you want it. Request pictures in addition to those posted, ask for room measurements (photos can be deceptive), probe for hidden costs, and try to pay with a credit card.

HOUSE SWAPS

Scores of French families are dying to swap houses with you during school vacation times—for nothing! Each of the following companies is largely Web-based and has listings that cover the world.

Intervac

The oldest and best-known house-swap outfit. The company publishes two annual catalogues for its members ($55 per copy, plus $95 one-year membership fee). Average number of listings: 10,000; 800/756-4663; intervac.com.

Homeexchange.com

This site offers the most exhaustive guidance for would-be swappers. Average number of listings: 6,500; 800/877-8723; annual fee $50.

Homelink International

This company produces a directory that members can receive twice a year for $45. Average number of listings: 14,000; 800/638-3841 or 954/566-2687; homelink.org; annual fee $75.

RENTAL PERIODS

Weekly rentals typically start on a Saturday and are often not ready until late afternoon. By the time you settle in, nearby stores will probably be closed until Monday, so pick up essentials en route. You can try asking the owner or manager to leave milk, bread, and coffee in the fridge.

TELEPHONES

Don't expect your house to have an answering machine. Use a phone card to make long-distance calls from there (France Télécom prepaid cards

The living room of the rental that Leslie Brenner chose for her clan.

can be good deals). If you must be reachable, rent or buy a tri-band GSM mobile phone, a global mobile phone that you can use in 210 countries. You'll also need a SIM card; French cards start at $69. Two-week rentals, with SIM-card and shipping, start at $142; if you already have a French (or International) SIM card, a two-week phone rental starts at $49.95. GSM-phone and SIM-card packages for purchase start at $160 through Planet Omni (877-327-5076; planetomni.com).

Leslie Brenner, snapping window details.

LANGOUSTINES
de CASIERS Bretagne
Le kg 2?3

MOULES
DE
BOUCHOTS
Le ,50 le LITRE

Shellfish at a Paris market.

Bistros of Provence

PROVENCE

NOTHING COMPARES TO A LANGUID LUNCH
OR A MULTICOURSE DINNER IN THE
COUNTRYSIDE, ESPECIALLY IN THE SOUTH
OF FRANCE. HERE, SOME OF THE REGION'S
MOST DELICIOUS RESTAURANTS.
BY LINDA DANNENBERG

One drizzly, bone-chilling week last winter I was in the Luberon, and the visit was not going well. Bad weather (yes, even in Provence) had caused work plans to go awry, leaving me with lost days and a grumpy disposition. For solace, I took myself to lunch at the cheerful Bistro de France in Apt. Within 20 minutes, planted on the *banquette* facing a truffle omelette and a generous glass of house *rouge*, I had an epiphany. I realized that at that moment, surrounded by animated diners and plumes of cigarette smoke, I felt utterly and completely happy. I hesitate to credit the bistro with transcendental powers, but that meal certainly brightened up my crummy day.

After that, in the course of writing a book on Provençal style, I traveled from Arles in the Rhône delta, through the mountainous Vaucluse, and eventually over to the Var, often in the company of my photographer, a *gourmand* who preferred to starve rather than face a *jambon* sandwich on the run. The noon to three o'clock slice of the day, when the light was often too harsh for photographs, provided the perfect opportunity for leisurely lunches in favorite old haunts as well as in some of the area's newest dining spots. Throughout our journey, I looked for the best local bistros, scoping out places that offered a Provençal *cuisine du marché*—olive oil–based cooking using fresh-from-the-market ingredients. The best places not only provided excellent food but also possessed the four basic characteristics of any good bistro: a distinct personality, intimacy, a convivial atmosphere, and a generous spirit. Here, plucked from our extended journey through the herb-scented landscape of the Midi, are a few favorites.

Photographs by Guy Bouchet

*Grilled vegetables at
La Charcuterie, in Arles.*

LA CHARCUTERIE, ARLES

On a narrow street opening onto the Place du Forum in the heart of old Arles, we found this former *charcuterie*, dating from 1942. The tiny space is now a winsome bistro with a modest décor of red velvet *banquettes* and pig figurines. The enterprise is fueled by the passion of François Colcombet, originally from Lyon, and his Arlesian wife, Regouya. Inspired by the tradition of the *bouchons lyonnais*—tiny bistros with hearty, sausage-based cuisine—François wanted to create a *bistro des copains* (bistro for friends), as he puts it. Regouya does all the cooking behind the original marble counter, in a space the size of a large sofa. The menu is a carnivore's dream, with main courses that showcase Charolais beef, rack of lamb, and grilled duck breast. (For vegetarians stranded here, Regouya is happy to whip up a platter of grilled Mediterranean vegetables, along with a crisp and garlicky mixed green salad.) I made a meal one night of the *charcuterie* platter, called the *assiette anglaise*, a lavish spread of cold cuts and a warm *saucisson de Lyon aux pistaches*, a mild sausage with chopped pistachio nuts in the filling. A dish this rich needs a dynamic red wine, and I splurged on two glasses of a 2000 Côte Rôtie. The pleasures of the inconspicuous Charcuterie have drawn many fans, among them the great foodie Jim Harrison, who chronicled his experience here in his memoir *Off to the Side*. Harrison might be amused to know that the Colcombets' chocolate Labrador retriever, Lanvin, has gnawed their copy of his book to shreds.

LE BISTROT DU PARADOU, LE PARADOU

I had many happy lunches at Chez Quénin, once a humble neighborhood canteen, while working on a book in the early eighties. Owners Jean-Louis and Mireille Pons, from nearby Arles, took over the restaurant shortly thereafter, changing the name to the trendier-sounding Bistrot du Paradou and improving the cuisine, while maintaining the character—vintage-tiled floors, stone walls, timbered ceilings—of the old place. Mireille, the daughter of an Arlesian baker, commands the open kitchen, while the personable Jean-Louis, with his wonderful Provençal accent (*vin blanc* becomes "*veng blahng*"), works the room. Just as in the days of Quénin, there is only a single four-course prix fixe at each meal. Tuesday, for example, might feature roasted farm-raised guinea hen, and Friday is the day for aioli, the traditional feast of steamed vegetables, salt cod, and local snails accompanied by the pungent garlic mayonnaise for which it is named. The price includes a bottle of wine—red, white, or rosé. My most recent dinner started with grilled orange

One of the meat platters offered at La Charcuterie, in Arles.

roughy fillets drizzled with olive oil and garnished with basil, followed by a main course of sliced leg of lamb served with a potato *gratin*. Dessert was Mireille's plump and flaky strawberry tart. "Our most faithful clients call us at the beginning of the week to find out the menus for the next five days," Jean-Louis says, "then plan their week accordingly."

LE BISTROT D'EYGALIÈRES, EYGALIÈRES

Does a restaurant with a Michelin two-star rating and a refined décor still merit the modest title of "bistro"? Yes, indeed, in the case of the Bistrot d'Eygalières, whose owners, the handsome young Belgian couple Suzy and Wout Bru, have maintained the true bistro spirit while offering a menu of exquisitely nuanced regional cuisine. This bistro de luxe, in a sleepy, out-of-the-way village a few miles south of the main road that runs between St.-Rémy and Cavaillon, has won over many high-profile neighbors: Charles Aznavour and Princess Caroline of Monaco frequently book tables, as do other members of the local *gratin*. Elegant and understated in tones of olive-gray and cream, the interior serves as background for Wout Bru's dazzling cuisine. Wout, an inventive chef, uses vinaigrette and jus bases to keep his cooking light and full of flavor. "I'm always looking for new ways to enhance the essence of each product I work with, from the farm, the forest, and the sea," he says. My mouth waters when I think back to my lavish lunch there, a medley of warm-lobster salad dressed with an earthy truffled vinaigrette; a *croustillant* (crisply grilled fillet) of baby pig, with savory and wild mushrooms; and a "gazpacho" of *fraises des bois*, tiny, fragrant wild strawberries.

NUMÉRO 75, AVIGNON

The former mansion of Jules Pernod, creator of the famous anisette liqueur that still bears his name, now houses a wonderful restaurant called Numéro 75. Noted local chef Robert Brunel, whose eponymous establishment, Brunel, faces the Palais des Papes, decided to take over the Pernod property to offer diners a more casual, countrified dining experience. Set behind an iron gate, 75 feels like a secret garden, fragrant with mimosa, bougainvillea, and lemon. "I wanted to create a bistro menu featuring simple Provençal cuisine and lots of salads," Brunel says, "dishes that are perfect for eating outdoors." He keeps his menus short, with only a handful of lunch and dinner choices. My alfresco meal on an evening in late spring—a silky foie-gras terrine studded with bits of poached artichoke hearts, followed by pan-roasted guinea hen paired with a tangy, tender lemon *confit*—was a delight. Salads, such as the combo of prosciutto, sun-dried tomato, and marinated eggplant, are popular with the after-theater crowd that fills the garden during Avignon's famous summer festival in July.

LE JARDIN DU QUAI, L'ISLE-SUR-LA-SORGUE

A lively group of antiques dealers surrounded me in the garden of Le Jardin du Quai, and all of us were eager to try chef Daniel Hebet's lunchtime specials. In a century-old house across from the train station in L'Isle-sur-la-Sorgue, a celebrated riverside town of antiquaires, Le Jardin du Quai is one of the best newer restaurants in Provence. Hebet, who drew rave notices as chef of the Hôtel La Mirande in Avignon, offers an unadorned but

Provençal figs.

The leafy courtyard at Jardin du Quai, in L'Isle-sur-la-Sorgue.

sophisticated market-based menu in an appropriate atmosphere of retro chic, complete with an old zinc bar and vintage bistro tables. On the afternoon I found myself seated under Hebet's vine-draped pergola, lunch started with a dish of grilled asparagus, shaved Parmesan, and fresh herbs. A tender, center-cut cod fillet on a bed of warm chickpeas flecked with orange zest was the main course; dessert was a luscious poached white peach in a cinnamon-spiked sugar syrup. The meal, enhanced by a golden Jean-Luc Colombo Les Figuières Côtes du Rhône, was unforgettable in its delicious understatement.

LE BOUQUET DE BASILIC, GORDES

In the tourist-clogged hill town of Gordes, it's not easy finding a place to eat—a pleasant, authentic, and reasonably priced place, that is, among the tourist canteens and the high-priced restaurants. Le Bouquet de Basilic, tucked behind a souvenir shop, is an adorable discovery. A leafy terrace offers cool shelter on a hot day, and the timbered, turmeric-hued interior is the perfect retreat when the mistral blows. Marianne Galante, the restaurant's amiable owner, has family roots in Sicily, and she has given a distinctly Mediterranean slant to her organic blackboard menu. Many dishes include Galante's glowingly fresh basil, the restaurant's namesake, as well as her locally pressed olive oil. I enjoyed the crab salad in a light, lemony vinaigrette, and my finicky photographer pronounced the tagliatelle with fresh tomatoes, basil, and garlic *très bon*. Our carafe of *rosé du pays*, the Fontenille Côtes du Luberon, dry and delicately fruity with a tiny hint of cranberry, was just right with this casual, southern-souled meal.

BISTRO DE FRANCE, APT

For me, this is the quintessential town bistro. Its individual elements (Formica tables, Naugahyde banquettes) may not be particularly attractive, but those motley parts add up to a beguiling whole. The restaurant has been spiffed up with a marbled trompe l'oeil façade, but it remains humble at heart. According to owner-chef Jackie André, the Bistro de France is one of the oldest in Provence, built where a bicycle shop and a café stood back in the twenties. The meals here are good the way the best home cooking is: fresh, unadorned, and generously served. There are black truffles in the winter, melons in the summer, and *cèpes* in the fall. With its seasonal specials and menu classics such as *crespéou*, a layered Provençal omelette with herbs, spinach, and zucchini, and old-fashioned *blanquette de veau*—the ultimate bistro comfort food—the Bistro de France always plays to a full house. The crowd chez Jackie is a congenial mix of local businessmen, happy tourists who happened to choose well, and real estate agents dragging along potential clients to show them a bit of local color. There is a daunting rush for tables after Apt's sprawling Saturday morning market, and disappointed shoppers are often turned away. Reserve!

*Rougets and tomato confit
at the Jardin du Quai.*

The produce and flower market in Aix-en-Provence. 113

Travelers' Guide to Western Provence

GETTING THERE

There are daily flights from Paris to Avignon, Marseilles, and Toulon, and the TGV Méditerranée rail link from Paris services both Avignon and Aix-en-Provence. For those with plenty of time, the A7 Autoroute du Soleil runs through western Provence en route to Marseilles.

EXPLORING WESTERN PROVENCE

At the mouth of the Rhône lie the flat, wetland marshes and sand dunes of the Camargue wildlife reserve. Farther inland, cities such as Avignon, Arles, and Aix-en-Provence are awash with ancient architecture. Northeast of Arles, the herb-covered chain of the Alpilles rises from the surrounding plains. Farther north still are the rugged limestone peaks of the Petit Luberon.

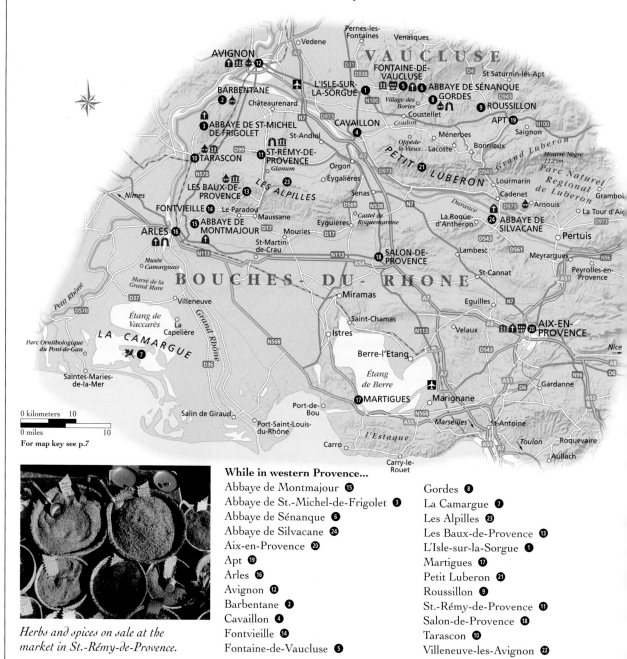

Herbs and spices on sale at the market in St.-Rémy-de-Provence.

While in western Provence...

Abbaye de Montmajour ⓯
Abbaye de St.-Michel-de-Frigolet ❸
Abbaye de Sénanque ❻
Abbaye de Silvacane ㉔
Aix-en-Provence ⓴
Apt ⓳
Arles ⓰
Avignon ⓬
Barbentane ❷
Cavaillon ❹
Fontvieille ⓮
Fontaine-de-Vaucluse ❺

Gordes ❽
La Camargue ❼
Les Alpilles ㉓
Les Baux-de-Provence ⓳
L'Isle-sur-la-Sorgue ❶
Martigues ⓱
Petit Luberon ㉑
Roussillon ❾
St.-Rémy-de-Provence ⓫
Salon-de-Provence ⓲
Tarascon ⓾
Villeneuve-les-Avignon ㉒

Apt's Bistro de France, packed on a sunny Saturday.

WHERE TO EAT

Bistro de France
67 Place de la Bouquerie, Apt;
33-4/90-74-22-01;
lunch for two $$;
losed Sundays and Mondays.

La Charcuterie
51 Rue des Arènes, Arles;
33-4/90-96-56-96;
dinner for two $$;
closed Sundays and all of August.

Le Bistrot d'Eygalières
Rue de la République, Eygalières;
33-4/90-90-60-34;
lunch for two $$$$;
open Tuesday evenings through
Sundays; closed November
through April.

Le Bistrot du Paradou
57 Ave. de la Vallée des Baux,
Le Paradou;
33-4/90-54-32-70;
dinner for two $$$;
closed Sundays and Mondays.

Le Bouquet de Basilic
Rte. de Murs, Gordes;
33-4/90-72-06-98;
lunch for two from $$$;
closed Wednesdays except in July
and August, when open daily.

Le Jardin du Quai
91 Ave. Julien-Guigue,
L'Isle-sur-la-Sorgue;

A salad of summer greens with artisanal olive oil at Bouquet de Basilic, in Gordes.

33-4/90-20-14-98;
danielhebet.com;
lunch for two $$$;
closed Tuesdays and Wednesdays.

Numéro 75
75 Rue Guillaume Puy, Avignon;
33-4/90-27-16-00;
dinner for two $$$;
open Tuesdays through Fridays,
Saturdays for dinner, and Mondays
for lunch; closed November
through April.

*The hill town of
Gordes, in Vaucluse.*

SEE ALSO
For more on Provence:
On the Wagon pp.66–67
New Wave Inns pp.94–95
Ma Vie en Rosé pp.150–151

Tastes of Brittany

A CULINARY TOUR OF NORTHWESTERN FRANCE YIELDS PRIZED OYSTERS, *FLEUR DE SEL*, AND AN ENCOUNTER WITH A CIDER MAKER WHO TREATS APPLES LIKE GRAPES BEING READIED FOR WINE. BY MATT LEE AND TED LEE

BRITTANY

Three wheels of butter like lumpy hassocks sat on a counter at Jean-Yves Bordier, the tiny, immaculate *fromagerie* hidden down a dark backstreet inside the walled city of St.-Malo. Although Bordier is an esteemed curator of cheeses, and France's best were shimmering on display by the dozens, the cashmere-draped ladies in line ahead of us had eyes only for the butter.

Two of the wheels were jasmine yellow, one marked DOUX, or "sweet," the other DEMI-SEL, or "salted." The third had no label and was flecked with green and lavender specks we took to be dried herbs. The man behind the counter, wielding a wooden paddle in each hand, pried a hefty chunk from the mammoth wheel of *demi-sel*, dropped it onto a sheet of waxed paper, and massaged it with his paddles into a small, tidy block, which he folded up in the paper and proffered to one of the women, who tucked it into her Goyard handbag and left.

And then it was our turn. We'd just driven four hours from Charles de Gaulle and were looking for a little something to spread on a baguette to tide us over until dinner. We summoned up our finest college French and a cool Jean Reno insouciance: "A quarter-kilo of the herb butter, please."

The man's face fell slightly. "It's not herb butter," he said. "I'm sorry. It's seaweed butter."

We nearly yelped with glee. Seaweed butter? We'd never before encountered *beurre aux algues*, but it seemed at once deeply old-world and strangely cutting-edge—exactly the sort of comestible we'd hoped to find when we set out for the windswept northwestern coast of France.

We'd been introduced to Brittany by a friend, Tom Moore, who'd spent his childhood summers in a farmhouse there and raved about its ocean-centric cuisine: a rustic, classic French, he had said, but with mystical influences thrown in—the enduring culinary legacy of the region's Celtic soul. During the Anglo-Saxon invasion of England, in the fifth and sixth centuries, some Britons sought asylum across the water, bringing their language, their rollicking music (heavy on harp and woodwinds), their traditional garb (including the *bigoudène*, a

distinctive tall headdress for women) to a land they called Breizh. France annexed the territory in the 16th century, but the Breton culture, language, and separatist instinct have endured.

There are precious few volumes on the dishes of Brittany, but we eventually found its bible: *Aimer la Cuisine de Bretagne* ("Loving the Cooking of Brittany"), by chef Jacques Thorel. The book included recipes for dishes with exotic-sounding names that only deepened our interest in the place. *Kig ha farz*, we learned, was the signature Breton dish, a meaty, dumpling-laced soup; *kouign amman* was a rich, sugary butter cake. The photographs showed food that looked both medieval (a furry, lifeless rabbit posed with a hunk of raw pork) and contemporary (a scattering of clams, each with its own airy cape of foam, that seemed to have emerged from a new-wave Barcelona kitchen). We were curious what form such a cuisine had taken in the new millennium.

So we charted a rough loop around Brittany, a broad peninsula that juts out toward England into the Atlantic. We would spend a couple of days in the northern fishing ports of St.-Malo and Cancale, then head southwest to Quimper, in the heart of cider-making country. We'd follow the region's southern coast east to the marshes of Guérande, source of the fabled *fleur de sel*, and circle back to Paris via Rennes, the Breton capital.

The seaweed butter was an early, favorable omen; spread on a fresh baguette, it had the sweet, creamy, salty flavor of a dense shellfish bisque. We had retreated from the tourist-choked streets of the walled city to the Chaussée du Sillon, a two-mile-long promenade overlooking the Gulf of St.-Malo, where locals were walking, bicycling, sunbathing, and kite boarding. We polished off our tartines on a narrow promontory that stretched so far into the shore break from the seawall that we felt we could reach out and touch the kite boarders launching themselves off the waves and into the air.

In their wet suits, against the backdrop of the ancient citadel, they resembled aliens from the

Photographs by Andrea Fazzari

Breton oysters, eaten throughout France.

future. And from where we stood, the promenaders watching from the seawall seemed to be paying homage to the waters that make Brittany the foremost supplier of fish and shellfish to the rest of the country. In fact, the region harvests nearly one-third of the oysters consumed in France, and much of its oystering industry is concentrated just 10 miles from St.-Malo, in Cancale—where we had a reservation for dinner.

As the sun dipped in the sky, we got back into our rented Citroën C2, a zippy modern take on the sixties' Deux Chevaux (and just as snail-like in appearance), and drove the coastal route east to Cancale. To our left, the craggy shoreline crept in and out of view as the road twisted and turned; to our right, we saw fields of hardy green leeks spiking out of the soil. We arrived close to dusk and dropped our bags at Château Richeux, an imposing grand manor just east of town, owned and managed by Olivier and Jane Roellinger, whose mini-empire, Les Maisons de Bricourt, includes two other deluxe lodgings and two food boutiques—Grain de Vanille, which sells handmade ice cream and pastries, and Épices Roellinger, a market stocking exotic spice blends and essential oils for cooking. Both shops serve as laboratories for the Roellinger kitchens,

The day's oyster harvest in Cancale.

among them a traditional seafood bistro in Château Richeux, and the more ambitious O. Roellinger, which Olivier runs out of his childhood home.

Olivier Roellinger was born and bred in Cancale, and he gets his culinary inspiration from the seafaring romance of his hometown. In publicity photos, he appears on the deck of a yacht, rugged and sea-sprayed, with the clenched look of an America's Cup mate executing a particularly challenging jibe. And he's prone to statements about food that beg to be uttered in that unctuous French-film-trailer voice: *I am ceaselessly creating new spice blends so that I can enrich the treasures of the earth and the sea.*

We walked into O. Roellinger somewhat wary, but our attention focused the moment the amuse-bouches—a sea snail bathed in an intense parsley water and a sweet shrimp dotted with microscopically diced tart apple—hit the table. In the similarly compelling pairings that followed—a grapefruit confit with turbot, a dab of sesame mayonnaise with tuna, an astoundingly floral nutmeg with baby sole—the oils and powders zinged across plates in artful dots and stripes were finely judged. As much as we wanted to mock the menu's breathless reference to "marine adventure," we had to admit: by channeling the spice-route corsairs who brought cardamom, curry, and cinnamon to this sleepy, windblown coast, Roellinger has created a stunning contemporary cuisine that occasionally soars out of this world.

A rural Breton landscape.

Another quintessential Breton experience awaited us the following morning, when we visited the clutch of stalls at the Cancale oyster market, on the seawall above Mont-St.-Michel Bay. The tide was low and the fog was in, but in the near distance we could make out a diesel tractor chuffing around the muddy oyster beds. The stalls were draped in striped canvas ticking in different shades of blue and run by women who shucked oysters to order and set them out on sturdy white plastic plates. We bought a dozen and sat on the seawall, spritzing lemon over them and slurping them down, and—as instructed by our friendly saleswoman—throwing the shells off the wall into the mud. They were glorious, unmistakably North Atlantic, with a sweet, cucumber-tinged brininess. It dawned on us that this snack was as nourishing to the senses as the previous evening's banquet— plus, it cost just $5, $300 less than we'd paid at O. Roellinger. We ordered another dozen, and by the time we'd finished, the haze over the bay had cleared; about 15 miles away, we saw Mont-St.-Michel, sitting on the opposite shore like a tiny Hershey's Kiss.

Rue Duguesclin in Cancale, home to the Roellingers' restaurant, shop, and hotel empire.

The tractor we'd been watching work the beds crept up a ramp in the seawall, dragging a trailerful of broad, flat bags of oysters, and we followed as it slowly made its way along the avenue that spanned the bayfront, stopping—and tying up traffic—every 100 yards or so to unload its catch at the town's bars.

So far, we hadn't uncovered much evidence of the *cuisine de Bretagne* we'd read about in Thorel. In St.-Malo, we'd tasted a few buttery, dense, but otherwise unremarkable sweet pastries labeled *kouign amman*. Road signs were bilingual—Breton and French—and we'd seen a spot of nationalist graffiti on a building near O. Roellinger (BZH: LA LIBERTÉ POUR BREIZH), but browsing menus in St.-Malo and Cancale, we'd found no trace of *kig ha farz*. Still, we continued to hope. Farther west, where we were headed, was Basse Bretagne, Lower Brittany, commonly known to have a more enduring Breton tradition. The towns along this southern coast, Tom had told us, were where we'd see women wearing *bigoudènes*.

Meanwhile, we were on our way to investigate the source of one Breton custom that did endure in St.-Malo and Cancale, judging from what we'd seen in the crêperies and oyster bars: the prodigious consumption of hard cider. Scores of people, young and old, drank cider, served in delicate ceramic teacups. We were eager to visit a cidery in southern Finistère, the heart of Brittany's cider-making region, so we hastened down major highways to Plonéis, just outside the town of Quimper, to drop in on Paul Coïc.

A young, first-generation cider maker, Coïc planted 1,600 apple trees on his parents' property in 1998 and is just now reaping the reward. Strolling the orchards, which roll out beyond the stone-walled barn that serves as his makeshift tasting room, Coïc plucked an apple from a tree and offered us a bite: it was so acrid, its relationship to the fruit we buy in the grocery store was hardly recognizable. The 12 varieties of apples tended by Coïc and his wife, Marie-Laurence, are of three general types, he told us—bitter, bittersweet, and sweet. His cider is made in much the same way wine is: he presses the juice by varietal and creates a blend, then ferments and ages it.

Many of Brittany's *cidreries* have been turned into appallingly commercial engines for generating tourist dollars; the Coïcs prefer to pour all their resources into the quality of their juice. Their work has paid off—their two ciders, a lovely champagne-like brut with a gingery note and a fuller-bodied, yeasty *doux*, are fabulous, and the Coïcs now supply bars and crêperies that specialize in authentic Breton food.

Coïc also offered us sips of *lambig*—a Breton spirit distilled from hard cider that has a burnt-caramel, rocket-fuel, and apple kick. We felt we must be getting closer to a Breton dining experience, so we asked Marie-Laurence if she knew of a restaurant that served *kig ha farz*. "Only one," she said. "Chez Erwan, near the train station in Quimper."

Before hitting Quimper, though, we had to take a short detour, toward the Pointe du Raz, as far west as you can go in France without running into the sea. In Cléden-Cap-Sizun, according to Tom, we'd find an old-fashioned seafood restaurant, L'Étrave, whose grilled lobster is something of a French legend. The place wasn't much to look at, but there was not an empty space in the parking lot—always a good sign. Inside, judging from the clientele, it might have been the dining hall of a prosperous nursing home.

And the lobster? Nothing more complicated than the freshest specimens split down the middle, sluiced with the heaviest cream, and scorched under a broiler to darken the edges of the meat and the surface of the cream. Served in an oval pan the size of a canoe, it was heaven plain and simple—so heavenly, we had to brace ourselves for the possibility that whatever delights awaited us would be an inevitable return to earth.

Quimper is a handsome town that straddles a river and is best known for its faïence, or glazed pottery, an industry founded on the banks of the canal in the late 17th century. Bypassing the modern food-market hall, we visited a small but nevertheless comprehensive museum on the site of a 1773 factory that effectively illustrates the modern history of Brittany through the evolving design of its tableware and clay figures. Our favorite pieces were those by René Quillivic, from early in the 20th century, showing Renaissance revivalism giving way to Art Deco and other modern influences.

That night, on a dark side street in downtown Quimper, we found Erwan. But first we ducked into Le Ceili, a friendly bar, to check out the loud music there, which sounded as if it came straight from the Scotch-Irish canon: panpipes and mandolin. Inside, we quaffed a couple of pints of Coreff, a tasty microbrew we'd seen advertised as *la première bière artisanale Bretonne*. The brewery was founded some 20 years ago; it has already become the Breton Guinness.

Across the street, Erwan beckoned, with its curiously lurid purple façade and bordello interior,

121

and in we went to seek our culinary quarry. Little did we know how lucky we were: *kig ha farz* is now on the daily menu, but at the time we visited, Erwan offered its *formule Breton*—a menu of either *kig ha farz* or *pesked farz du* (a dish of sea bream and dumplings), followed by a Breton dessert—only on Tuesdays, or by reservation. It just happened to be Tuesday, and we were even so fortunate as to get the very last portion of *kig ha farz*, the rustic stew of assorted meats and buckwheat dumplings traditionally served in two stages. We watched as a table of three received their bowls: the local couple schooled their novice guest in how the dish is eaten. Erwan, the chef-owner, kindly helped us.

First, a beefy, almost cola-colored broth arrived in a glass bowl, with bread for dipping and a spoon for slurping. Then an oval faïence platter—crowded with slab bacon, pork shank, beef shoulder steak, and a hefty marrowbone—hit the table with a thud. Only later did we discover the layer of vegetables underneath—big chunks of roasted carrot and patty-shaped dumplings. A pitcher of hot clarified butter flavored with onion cracklings was served alongside, to lubricate the feast.

This 19th-century plowman's supper seemed fondue-like in its frank separation of protein and oil, and yet it didn't ring true as "French." As with any comfort food, we wondered what shape it might take in the hands of an imaginative chef who had the power to both channel and elevate the local grub. Would Jacques Thorel be that chef? If we could work up our appetites in the next 12 hours, we would try to find out.

Driving farther south along the coast, we came to La Roche-Bernard, a former trading post on a bluff overlooking the river Vilaine. We strolled through town, killing time before our lunch reservation chez Thorel, dropping in on the studio of a mosaicist and the gallery of an accomplished potter, both located in a complex of former granaries. The 17th-century Auberge Bretonne, an elegant half-timbered stone edifice in the center of town, boasts some of the most luxurious lodgings in Brittany. There's a suave *richesse* to the Thorel dining room: stone floors, warmly colored stucco walls, Villeroy & Boch table settings, Spiegelau stemware. We were seated next to the glassed-in orangerie, open to the sky, that contains the restaurant's kitchen garden, which brimmed with the darkest earth and healthiest plants we'd seen in years. Beans raced up their poles; tomatoes beamed.

There were two menus on offer: one, an homage to the fabled sweet winemaker Château d'Yquem, paired a half bottle of 1993 d'Yquem with classic French fare such as lobster cooked in Sauternes. The chef's tasting menu—strongly recommended by our waiter—would show Thorel's more contemporary compositions, or *nouveautés*. Feeling adventurous, we opted for the latter, and out came seven amuse-bouches, a collection of small shot glasses and tiny plates, each more confounding than the one before. There was a mousse-like mustard wrapped in a peanut-brittle "taco," and a beet jelly so overgelled that a spoon was of little use. The next course, "*quelques légumes de notre jardin*," consisted of seven more tastes we were thankful were small—the asparagus flan was covered in too-crunchy coffee nibs. And so it went, the novelties arriving at the

Harvesting fleur de sel *in Guérande.*

The 25-seat Table d'Eugénie, in Rennes.

table with wonderful visual ceremony and yet underwhelming flavors. At a neighboring two-top, the stocky businessmen who'd ordered the menu of *classiques*, a gorgeous lobster *en cocotte* and a bottle of Château d'Yquem, leaned back with satisfaction. The past never looked so good—and the future looked expensive; our lunch for two (with wine) came to more than $500. We should have used Thorel's terrific book as our guide to his kitchen and stuck to the simple, the traditional. Brittany is no place for tacos.

It was time to get back to the basics. Next stop, the salt flats. By the time we reached Guérande, we were so transfixed by the marshy landscape that our lunch disappointment was a distant memory. On an impossibly intricate field, as far as the eye could see, were geometric enclosures of open water inscribed with mazelike channels, where the *paludiers*, or salt panners, evaporate the salty Atlantic into an even saltier conclusion. A few narrow roads traverse the green swaths of marsh that surround the pans, and we drove right through the middle of the field until we came across a panner selling bags of discounted *fleur de sel*, the finest grade of feather-light crystals. We bought as much as we could fit into the little Citroën.

We traveled on to Rennes, a busy university town with an old quarter of densely clustered half-timbered houses that seem to lean precariously against one another and to teeter over the narrow *ruelles*. Running along the lintels of the finer houses are delicately carved reliefs of warriors and saints— we thought we saw one figure carrying a salt pan. We were out crêperie-hopping, downing cider by the teacup, when we came across a short, sturdy guy in a chef's apron posting a new menu in the window of a whitewashed room with 12 tables. We took a closer look and read: *I propose a menu that evolves over the months. With a menu this short, I can offer you the best of each ingredient.*

The chef's tasting menu was $51. It seemed like a direct challenge to us, so we made a reservation for that night and pledged to stop eating crêpes.

Our dinner at La Table d'Eugénie was the most contemporary meal we experienced during the whole trip: pretty, full of intense, seasonal flavors, stylishly spiced (just enough to seem original), minimalist without being mannered. A dense, silky terrine of foie gras was shaped and toned by the sweet fire of five-spice powder down one side and a sprinkling of crackly *fleur de sel*. A single seared scallop on a pillow of pearl barley had creamy tomato gravy with a hint of fenugreek and a wisp of lemon zest. Pig's cheeks, cooked to melting tenderness in a

rich Armagnac and pork broth for seven hours, were served in a cast-iron Staub pot with snappy summer peas, leeks, baby squash, new potatoes, and a tender carrot, a latter-day *kig ha farz*.

Toward the end of the night, the chef emerged, in a white T-shirt and sneakers, and passed from table to table to introduce himself. He was Erwann Hergué, not a Quimper local but a native of St.-Nazaire, near Guérande; he was relatively new in town; his restaurant had opened in December 2003.

And before that? we asked.

He'd been working at a place called Jean Georges, he said, in New York City—had we heard of it?

Rang a bell, we said.

Actually, he hadn't been a chef there, only a service captain, but he picked up a few tricks observing what went on in the kitchen before his work visa ran out. He had a hunch that he'd return to Brittany someday, to open the place of his dreams—nothing complicated or expensive, just straightforward cooking, but fresh in its own way. We thanked him profusely for finishing our trip on that perfect note, and promised we'd give his regards to Broadway.

Hearty pork cheek and seasonal vegetable stew at La Table d'Eugénie.

Travelers' Guide to Brittany

WHEN TO GO

Many of Brittany's best hotels and restaurants close for the winter months, so the prime time to visit is April through October (with the exception of August, the French national holiday, when the region is overcrowded).

GETTING THERE

Brittany's easternmost edge is a four-hour drive from Paris. The fastest route to Breton towns is to fly from Paris on Air France to Rennes's St.-Jacques airport (RNS), then rent a car.

EXPLORING BRITTANY

Ideal for a seaside vacation, Brittany offers enjoyable drives along the headlands and beaches of the northern Côte d'Emeraude and Côte de Granit Rose, the south coast boasts wooded valleys and the stunning prehistoric sites of Carnac and the Golfe du Morbihan. Make sure you also visit the charming cathedral town of Quimper; the regional capital, Rennes; and the great castle at Fougères. In summer, take a boat trip to one of Brittany's tranquil islands.

While in Brittany...
Belle-Île-en-Mer ㉑
Brest ❷
Cancale ㉘
Carnac ⑲
Combourg ㉚
Concarneau ❾
Côte d'Émeraude ㉖
Côte de Granit Rose ⑯
Dinan ㉙
Douarnenez ❹
Forêt de Paimpont ㉕
Fougères ㉜
Golfe du Morbihan ㉓
Guimiliau ⑭
Île de Bréhat ⑱
Île d'Ouessant ❶
Josselin ㉔
Lampaul-Guimiliau ⑮
Le Pouldu ⑪
Locronan ❺
Parc Naturel Régional d'Amorique ❸
Pays Bigouden ❼
Pointe du Raz ❻
Pont-Aven ❿
Presqu'île de Quiberon ⑳
Quimper ❽
Rennes ㉛
Roscoff ⑫
St.-Malo ㉗
St.-Thégonnec ⑬
Tréguier ⑰
Vannes ㉒
Vitré ㉝

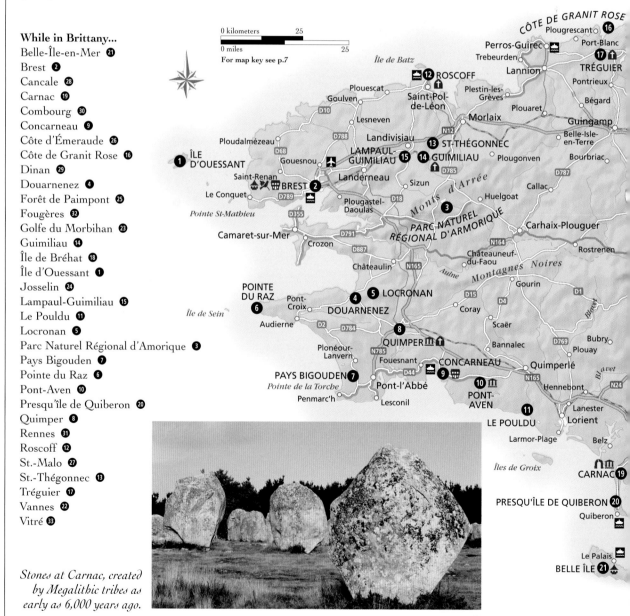

Stones at Carnac, created by Megalithic tribes as early as 6,000 years ago.

On the beach at Dinard, a classic seaside
resort on the Côte d'Émeraude.

WHERE TO STAY

Château de Locguénolé
*An elegant 18th-century estate just south
of Quimper, and steps from the sea.*
Route de Port Louis en Kervignac,
Hennebont;
33-2/97-76-76-76;
chateau-de-locguenole.com;
doubles from ⓈⓈ.

Hostellerie du Moulin de Rosmadec
*This quaint four-room hotel — which
also has one apartment for rent — rises on
a riverbank in Pont-Aven, an artists'
haven Gauguin visited regularly in the
late 1880's.*
Venelle de Rosmadec, Pont-Aven;
33-2/98-06-00-22;
doubles from Ⓢ.

L'Auberge Bretonne
*Chef Jacques Thorel's wife,
Solange, runs an inn above his
restaurant, with spacious rooms
that exude old-money polish
and clubby charm.*
2 Place Duguesclin,
La Roche-Bernard;
33-2/99-90-60-28;
auberge-bretonne.com;
doubles from ⓈⓈ.

Château de Fougères, a
superb example of medieval
military architecture.

Buckwheat crêpe and cider, at Douarnenez's Crêperie de la Passerelle.

Lecoq-Gadby
A pretty, century-old 11-room inn in a residential neighborhood.
156 Rue de Antrain, Rennes;
33-2/99-38-05-55;
lecoq-gadby.com;
doubles from $$.

Les Maisons de Bricourt
Olivier and Jane Roellinger offer rooms in a grand 1920's villa; a stately, ivy-covered stone house; or renovated seamen's cabins.
1 Rue Duguesclin, Cancale;
33-2/99-89-64-76;
maisons-de-bricourt.com;
doubles from $$.

Manoir de Lan-Kerellec
The chic manor house-hotel has a Michelin-starred restaurant and overlooks the islands off the northern

Granit Rosé coast.
Allée Centrale de Lan-Kerellec, Trébeurden;
33-2/96-15-00-00;
lankerellec.com;
doubles from $$.

WHERE TO EAT
Maison du Voyageur O. Roellinger
Brittany's star chef Olivier Roellinger transforms the region's raw materials into contemporary haute cuisine.
1 Rue Duguesclin, Cancale;
33-2/99-89-64-76;
dinner for two $$$$$.

Le Chalut
Don't let the campy sea-shanty décor fool you; the kitchen prepares delicious dishes

Seaweed butter at Jean-Yves Bordier, St.-Malo's master beurrier.

from the bounty of the local waters.
8 Rue de la Corne du Cerf, St.-Malo;
33-2/99-56-71-58;
dinner for two $$.

Au Pied de Cheval
The market near the docks at Cancale offers the ur–oyster experience. This is the best of the bayfront oyster houses.
10 Quai Gambetta, Cancale;
33-2/99-89-76-95;
dinner for two $$.

Crêperie de la Passerelle
Set above the docks of the pretty port town of Douarnenez, this crêperie serves authentic buckwheat pancakes.
17 Blvd. Camille Réaud, Douarnenez;
33-2/98-92-13-28;
lunch for two $.

L'Étrave
The legendary creamed lobster served in this vaulted, no-frills dining room, not far from Brittany's blustery Baie des Trépassés, is not to be missed.
Rte. de la Pointe du Van, Cléden-Cap-Sizun;
33-2/98-70-66-87;
dinner for two $$$$.

Erwan
Beneath the wacky skin of this bistro lies a beating Breton heart. The chef cooks rib-sticking dishes like kig ha farz, a landlubber's bouillabaisse.
1–3 Rue Aristide Briand, Quimper;
33-2/98-90-14-14;
dinner for two $$.

La Gaillotière

South of Nantes, Olivier Roellinger protégé Benoît Debailly serves French country cuisine with flashes of modern brilliance.
Château Thébaud;
33-2/28-21-31-16;
dinner for two $ $.

La Table d'Eugénie

Young chef-owner Erwann Hergué brings meticulous technique to simple, fresh French food.
2 Rue des Dames, Rennes;
33-2/99-30-78-18;
dinner for two $ $ $.

WHAT TO DO

Cidrerie Paul Coïc

Five miles northwest of Quimper, a first-generation cider maker produces top-notch brews and distilled lambigs.
Kerscouédic, Plonéis;
33-2/98-91-14-11.

Musée de la Faïence de Quimper

This compact museum brings to life the 300-plus years of artisanal glazed-ware production in Quimper.
14 Rue Jean-Baptiste Bousquet, Quimper;
33-2/98-90-12-72;
quimper-faiences.com.

Musée des Marais Salants

After chatting with salt panners in the marshes of Guérande, learn how their ancestors harvested the world's finest salt.
29 bis Rue Pasteur, Batz-sur-Mer;
33-2/40-23-82-79.

Oan's Pub

The Celtic origins of Breizh are audible in the rollicking Friday-night live music sessions at this pub, which is also serious about local beers.
1 Rue Georges Dottin, Rennes;
33-2/99-31-07-51.

WHAT TO READ

Aimer la Cuisine de Bretagne
By Jacques Thorel.
Not available in English, this outstanding guide to the region's cuisine includes recipes and stunning photographs throughout.

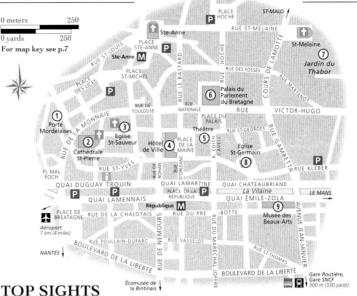

TOP SIGHTS IN RENNES

Cathédrale de St.-Pierre ❷

The cathedral stands on what's been the site of Christian worship since the 6th century. Although it retains its 16th-century façade, St.-Pierre was rebuilt from 1784.

Basilique St.-Sauveur ❸

An 18th-century church where the composer Gabriel Fauré was organist.

Église St.-Germain ❽

This church, which reflects the opulence of the haberdashers' parish in the 16th-century, has a typical Breton belfry and wooden vaulting.

Hôtel de Ville ❹

Built by Jacques Jules Gabriel after the great fire of 1720, the town hall consists of two wings framing the Baroque belfry.

Jardins du Thabor ❼

Once part of a Benedictine monastery, these attractive gardens are ideal for walks and picnics.

Musée des Beaux Arts ❾

This collection of art ranges from the 14th century to the present. It features a room dedicated to art on Breton themes, including work by Gaugin, Bernard, and other members of the Port-Aven school.

Palais du Parlement du Bretagne ❻

The 17th-century Breton parliament building now houses the law courts. The structure was restored to its former splendour after a fire in 1994.

Portes Mordellaises ❶

These ceremonial gates were the main gateway through which kings, dukes, and bishops entered the city.

Théâtre de Rennes ❺

In designing this theater as a rotunda with arcades and covered alleyways, the architect, Charles Millardet, attempted to create a building that would also function as a meeting place and a center of trade.

Medieval houses in Rennes.

129

A misty morning at Château de la Treyne, a hotel overlooking the Dordogne River.

Back to the Land

DORDOGNE

IF A FRENCHMAN'S HEART LIVES IN PARIS, HIS STOMACH RESIDES IN THE DORDOGNE, WHERE UNEARTHING THE REGION'S FLAVORS MEANS DIGGING INTO DUCK CONFIT, FOIE GRAS, AND GOAT CHEESE. BY LESLIE BRENNER

A restaurant opening in France's Dordogne Valley has nothing in common with one in Paris or New York. Instead of a gaggle of reviewers and industry insiders, you're more likely to find a roomful of farmers, bakers, florists, and children. At the decidedly unglamorous debut of La Ferme de Berle, a farm-restaurant near Collonges-la-Rouge, one relaxed spring evening, my husband and I sat on plastic chairs sipping homemade *vin de noix*, walnut aperitif. Through the room's picture windows we could see cows grazing in the pasture. At a long table for eight, an organic-beef farmer chatted excitedly with a postal worker; a shoe merchant and the town *pharmacienne* shared a tureen of *choucroute garnie*. Outside, Salomé, the chef's little daughter, played with her dog and greeted familiar faces.

I was introduced to the Dordogne Valley of southwestern France, which includes the culinary region of Périgord, by Danièle Mazet-Delpeuch,

Just-picked cèpes *and spinach.*

Danièle Mazet-Delpeuch in the kitchen of La Borderie, an inn where she operates a cooking school, in St. Martin de Coux.

formerly palace chef to François Mitterrand. I had met Danièle in New York, and she had invited me to visit her family's 700-year-old stone farmhouse. I was tantalized by Danièle's descriptions of the countryside, the ancient villages built into the steep cliffs along the Dordogne River, the imposing châteaux and simple Romanesque churches, the well-preserved *bastides*, or fortified towns. But what intrigued me most was the food: truffles, *cèpes* (porcini), walnut oil and *vin de noix*, the renowned goat cheese *cabécou* (fresh and mild, with a soft rind and creamy center) and, of course, ducks and geese and their foie gras.

The moment I arrived, I fell in love. Everything I tasted seemed like the best thing I'd ever eaten. And Danièle was the perfect host—more than just a devoted gourmande, she's an expert on every aspect of the region's food, and she was generous with her knowledge. Once, as we drove back to her farm in the late afternoon on a one-lane mountain road, Danièle slammed on the brakes, walked around to the front of her tiny, beat-up Renault, and returned holding her prize by the ears: roadkill. The rabbit, she announced, was still warm and would make a marvelous pâté.

Some 10 years later I was back on that same road, this time accompanied by my husband, Thierry. I

had returned to the Dordogne to seek out the region's best food, and aimed to enlist the help of my old friend.

In her lilac-scented garden, Danièle served us tea and *pain de miel* (honey cake) and talked of the cooking courses she offers that celebrate the region's cuisine. Intense and fiery, she is also a solid, earthy woman of the *terroir* who calls herself "just a grandmother filled with recipes." Teaching cooking is nothing new to Danièle—she was one of the originators of the "foie gras weekends" popular in the 1970's, when foreign tourists and vacationing Parisians would come to spend a couple of days down on the farm.

Where could we get a great meal? "You're in luck," she said. "A friend of mine—*une vraie cuisinière*—is opening her farm-restaurant just outside Collonges tonight." For Danièle to call someone *une vraie cuisinière*, a real cook, was a tremendous compliment.

As we drove through the countryside, I was overwhelmed by the region's natural beauty. I remembered feeling the same way on my first visit. The landscapes leaned more toward the sublime than the subtle, with dramatic limestone gorges; curious loops in the river, called *cingles*, that bend in almost complete circles; and endless old-growth forests. It is a place that feels older than ancient, where the medieval châteaux forts seem but recent history next to the plentiful prehistoric sites.

A façade in Domme, one of France's Most Beautiful Villages.

Collonges-la-Rouge, a village built almost entirely from red sandstone, may just be the most beautiful spot in France. The setting sun cast a rosy glow on the village's red stones as we took a walk to admire the towered and turreted manor houses, the narrow footpaths, and the handful of artisanal shops. Collonges is one of the 149 Most Beautiful Villages in France, a collection of villages scattered across the countryside that have been selected for their beauty, architecture, and historic interest. It was founded in the eighth century around a church and priory, but what you see today dates mostly from the 11th to the 16th centuries. We were surprised to have the town almost entirely to ourselves—a benefit of visiting off-season. After checking into the only hotel in Collonges, we headed for Danièle's friends' farm.

Unlike other "farm-restaurants" we'd been to, La Ferme de Berle really is a working farm—raising cattle and producing walnut products. The chef, Laurence Salvant, whose magenta-streaked hair marked her as a city girl (she's Parisian), greeted us warmly at the door. Her husband emerged from the kitchen in a denim apron covered with flour, having spent the day making bread. Jean-Jacques is a dark-skinned fellow with apple cheeks; his family has owned the farm since "*seize cents et quelques*" ("sixteen hundred–something").

We took our seats—next to the postal worker and the farmer—and accepted glasses of the house-made *vin de noix*. Along with these came a plate of

Camembert in a brioche croûte *at La Ferme de Berle.*

hors d'oeuvres that Laurence called "*tartes berloises*": *grattons* (crisp duck skin), crème fraîche, walnuts, and bacon baked onto bread. Their salty richness was complemented by the velvety, sweet wine.

Choucroute à la Laurence came next, a mountain of tender sauerkraut made from cabbage grown on the farm, garnished with succulent sausages, steamed potatoes that tasted as though they'd just been pulled from the earth, and, for an iconoclastic Perigordian touch, a flavorful *confit de canard*. We sopped it all up hungrily with yet more thick slabs of delicious bread.

Later, Laurence joined us for a glass of wine. Until now, she'd never cooked professionally, but she had long dreamed of opening a small-scale restaurant at home. "A friend said she had a cousin who was living alone on a farm," Laurence told us, "and he wanted to do meals there." They met, and when Jean-Jacques taught Laurence his grandfather's method of making bread in the wood-burning oven, she knew this must be love; they married soon after.

Much to our surprise, the extraordinary meal, including a decent bottle of wine, was only about $60. Delighted with the bargain, we put down a credit card. It took a few minutes before we realized that, of course, they didn't accept plastic. We promised to return the next morning with cash. Good thing they didn't make us wash dishes for our supper: the next day, Laurence told us she and Jean-Jacques had stayed awake washing up past 2 a.m.

Jean-Jacques Salvant emerged from the kitchen in a denim apron covered with flour, having spent the day making bread

Jean-Jacques Salvant carries freshly baked bread at La Ferme de Berle, a farm-restaurant in Collonges-la-Rouge.

135

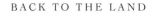

As wonderful as our farm supper had been, we still craved a superlative four-course meal; though we'd arrived more than a week before, we had yet to find one. Some good meals, yes—foie gras served three ways at Le Relais des Cinq Châteaux, a modest restaurant in a hotel that stood amid corn and tobacco fields. Fat white and green asparagus in a balsamic vinaigrette dotted with *lentilles de Puy* at La Meynardie, a charming spot where we sat on the shady terrace of what was no longer a working farm. And, most notably, a picnic in La Roque-Gageac, made from ingredients purchased at the fantastic market in nearby Sarlat.

Danièle offered to make us dinner, but I demurred (though I'm still kicking myself); I was bent on finding an extraordinary restaurant. We found one at Château de la Treyne, a graceful Relais & Châteaux property whose buildings date from the 14th and the 17th century respectively. The hotel is set on a storybook-perfect site over the river near the village of Lacave.

The château's 16 rooms are elegantly furnished, with jewel-toned brocades. Ours, named Henri IV, had an antique four-poster and looked out over the formal gardens. When we sat down to dinner, the room was bathed in the light of the sunset reflected off the river; the owner walked through, lighting candles. I started with a terrine of duck foie gras, accompanied by a purée of figs and an intense *gelée* flavored with Monbazillac, a sweet white wine. Since the region is famous for lamb, I couldn't pass up the fillet roasted with mustard and thyme and served with the kidneys. Thierry chose a *chartreuse de pigeonneau du Sud-Ouest* with truffle juice. The chef played up the natural gaminess of the bird, serving it rare with the foie gras; buttery Savoy cabbage was the perfect garnish.

The wine list was a gold mine for Bordeaux lovers. We selected a 1995 Château Beychevelle—redolent of fruit and beguilingly complex. With wine remaining in our glasses, the cheese trolley was irresistible. After that, the *corne d'abondance*—a puff pastry with a *confit* of the ripest berries, *fromage blanc* ice cream, and a *coulis* of Muscat de Rivesaltes—was altogether light, bright, and ethereal.

Our dinner at Château de la Treyne was as formal as La Ferme's was rustic. The only sign of chef Stéphane Andrieux came the next morning as we pulled out of the gravel-lined parking lot. The door to the pretty blue-and-white-tiled kitchen was open, revealing Andrieux and his small team starting work on that evening's dinner.

Château de la Treyne, near Lacave.

137

I found the earthy Périgord cooking of my dreams in *bastide* country, about a half-hour drive west of Lacave, in Monpazier. Founded in 1285 by Edward I of England, Monpazier is one of the region's most striking fortified towns: I was immediately won over by its geometric beauty. In contrast to other members of the Most Beautiful Villages, this was a functioning town, with appliance stores, shoe-repair shops, and a weekly outdoor market.

The day we arrived, the market filled the square; farmers, cheesemongers, and *charcutiers* had come from every corner of the valley. At one stall, two young men in jeans sold *saucissons secs*—dried sausages made from pork, boar, or rabbit. "*Goûtez, goûtez!*" they shouted, holding out samples on the ends of their pocketknives. I recognized one cheesemonger from the market at Sarlat; he was hawking his wares from behind a wheeled dairy case that held flats of ash-covered logs and aged, hockey-puck-sized disks of *cabécou*. On the far side of the market were the fishmonger and butcher, and farm stands filled with neatly stacked white asparagus, bunches of tomatoes on the vine, and baskets of perfumed strawberries. Nearby, a group of old men in berets gossiped and argued.

Now that our appetites were piqued, I asked the concierge at our low-key hotel if she could recommend a restaurant for dinner.

That evening, crossing the now-empty square, we entered a narrow side street paved with cobblestones and lined with shops more utilitarian than touristy. We walked into La Bastide to find a table in the bar filled with locals, all of whom seemed to be friends of the house. Huge vases of roses and Queen Anne's lace cheered up the slightly dowdy, pink-tablecloth dining room; copper pots and bowls hung on the walls. When I asked for the four-course *saveur du terroir* menu, the waitress's mouth turned up in a half-smile; she was pleased that I was ready for the full experience.

My first course, the *foie gras frais au torchon*—an expertly seasoned duck liver—was rich and velvety, perfectly smooth. Then came an admirable *omelette aux cèpes*. The mushrooms, cooked slowly in goose fat, were silky, soft, and plump. *Confit de canard* was next, deeply flavorful, with golden-brown skin, and garnished with diced potatoes sautéed in garlic and more goose fat. After *salade à l'huile de noix* and just-ripe *cabécou*, who could even consider dessert?

The back of the menu listed chef Gérard Prigent's artisanal producers: chickens from Durou farm in Rampieux, ducks from La Quercynoise in

Fresh vegetables for sale in Monpazier.

Bundled white asparagus at market.

Périgueux, completed its renovation in 2007, but Michelin-starred chef Philippe Etchebest began the transformation process six years earlier when he introduced a lighter, more refined version of traditional Perigordian cuisine in the Château's restaurant, L'Oison. Under the direction of the new chef, Gilles Gourvat, L'Oison's menu has remained the same, offering seasonal delights, which, when we visited, included a delicate ravioli of langoustine in a frothy cream sauce atop julienned cucumbers tinged with cumin and lasagne of seared foie gras and wild mushrooms heightened by an extravagant black truffle emulsion. The sleek tableware from Spain—a white Bidasoa porcelain plate with an oversized rim and a teacup-sized depression in the center—contrasts with the restaurant's crystal chandeliers and heavy red curtains, an interplay of contemporary and classic styles that is echoed in the post-renovation decor of the rest of the Château. The redone rooms are whimsical (Louis XV chairs upholstered in tangerine-hued crushed velvet), and play on local themes (the Dordogne room has furniture made from sticks and rocks). They were also more stylish and appealing than anything else we'd seen in the Dordogne; five euros says this witty take on traditional style, along with an updated version of classic cuisine, becomes the region's next big thing.

Gramat, *verjus* from Domaine de Siorac in St.-Aubin-de-Cabelech. I hadn't seen this kind of producer credit on any other menu in the region. Intrigued, we returned the next morning to have a chat with the chef. As it turned out, Prigent is the only chef in the Dordogne to have received official certification from the Ministry of Tourism as *Les Cuisineries Gourmandes des Provinces Françaises*, which requires members to use traditionally produced ingredients of the region in 70 percent of their dishes.

Over espressos, Prigent told us how he happened upon Monpazier more than 30 years ago. He had stopped for a drink at a café, and after soaking up the atmosphere, said to the waiter, "It's beautiful here—do a lot of people come through?" The waiter said, "Yes, but the problem is we don't have even one restaurant." The young chef was inspired to open La Bastide. Today Monpazier has a population of approximately 500, and eight restaurants.

Monpazier isn't the only town in the Dordogne whose restaurant scene has improved. The 19th-century Château des Reynats, just outside

Rocamadour goat cheese (also known as cabécou).

Travelers' Guide to the Dordogne

WHEN TO GO

Spring and early fall are the best times to visit this area. In May, the Dordogne is resplendent with lilacs and wisteria; white asparagus and strawberries are irresistible. *Cèpes* are in abundance on restaurant menus in the fall (though many establishments close for winter in early November). Summer is lovely too but French vacationers know that, and you will find them there in great number.

GETTING THERE

From North America, fly to Paris and connect to either Bergerac or Périgueux. A car is a must for seeing the best of the region. Get good maps (we suggest Michelin); the smallest roads are the most beautiful, but navigating them can be a challenge.

EXPLORING THE DORDOGNE

From the deep, narrow gorges of the Vézère to the fertile plains of the wide Dordogne Valley, the Périgord is a land of contrasts. The varied landscape is dotted with medieval villages, massive castles, and painted caves—traces of human activity dating back to prehistoric times.

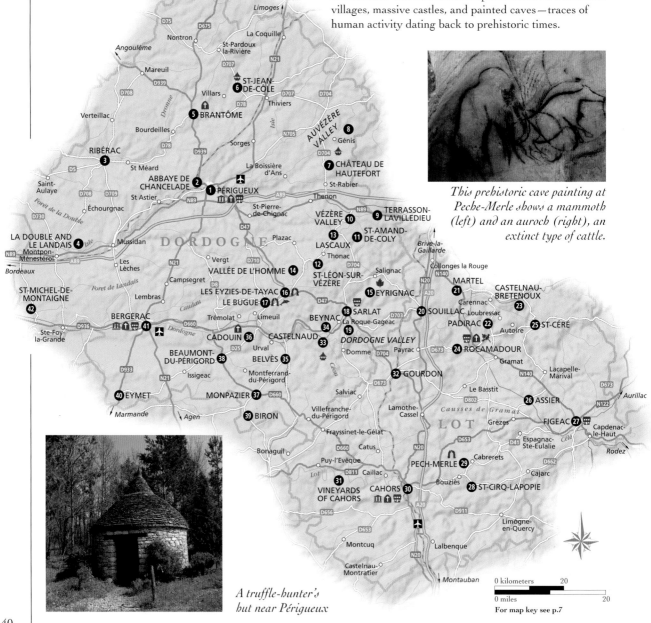

This prehistoric cave painting at Peche-Merle shows a mammoth (left) and an auroch (right), an extinct type of cattle.

A truffle-hunter's hut near Périgueux

0 kilometers 20

0 miles 20

For map key see p.7

While in the Dordogne...
Abbaye de Chancelade [2]
Assier [26]
Auvézère Valley [8]
Beaumont-du-Périgord [38]
Belvès [35]
Bergerac [41]
Beynac [34]
Biron [39]
Brantôme [5]
Cadouin [36]
Cahors [30]
Castelnau-Bretenoux [23]
Castelnaud [33]
Château de Hautefort [7]
Dordogne Valley [19]
Eymet [40]
Eyrignac [15]
Figeac [27]
Gourdon [32]
La Double and Le Landais [4]
Lascaux [13]
Le Bugue [17]
Les Ezyies-de-Tayac [16]
Martel [21]
Monpazier [37]
Padirac [22]
Pech-Merle [29]
Périgueux [1]
Ribérac [3]
Rocamadour [24]
St.-Amand-de-Coly [11]
St.-Céré [25]
St.-Cirq-Lapopie [28]
St.-Jean-de-Côle [6]
St.-Léon-sur-Vézère [12]
St.-Michel-de-Montaigne [42]
Sarlat [18]
Souillac [20]
Terrasson-Lavilledieu [9]
Vallee de l'Homme [14]
Vézère Valley [10]
Vineyards of Cahors [31]

WHERE TO STAY

Château de la Treyne
Located on 300 acres of parkland and forest, the château has 14 elegant rooms.
Lacave;
33-5/65-27-60-60;
chateaudelatreyne.com;
doubles from $$.

Château des Reynats
A renovation completed in 2007 made this formerly run-down castle arguably the most stylish hotel in the region.
Ave. des Reynats, Chancelade-Périgueux;
33-5/53-03-53-59;
chateau-hotel-perigord.com;
doubles $$ in the château, $ in the château annex.

Hôtel Edward 1er
A 19th-century manor house with small but charmingly furnished rooms.
5 Rue St.-Pierre, Monpazier;
33-5/53-22-44-00;
hoteledward1er.com;
doubles from $.

WHERE TO EAT

Ferme de Berle
Dine on family recipes at the farm of Laurence and Jean-Jacques Salvant.
Berle, Collonges-la-Rouge;
33-5/55-25-48-06;
dinner for two $$.

Le Relais des Cinq Châteaux
Unpretentious, traditional Périgord cooking.
Vézac-en-Périgord;
33-5/53-30-30-72;
dinner for two $$.

Restaurant La Meynardie
Three- to five-course menus served on the pretty terrace of a farmhouse.
Paulin, Salignac-Eyvigues;
33-5/53-28-85-98;
dinner for two $$$.

The village of Monpazier.

Château de la Treyne
Chef Stéphane Andrieux's refined dishes shine in this romantic setting.
Lacave;
33-5/65-27-60-60;
dinner for two $$$$.

Restaurant La Bastide
Traditional Dordogne specialties. Don't miss the foie gras au torchon.
52 Rue St.-Jacques, Monpazier;
33-5/53-22-60-59;
dinner for two $$$.

L'Oison
Gilles Gourvat's innovative dishes are the valley's most pleasant culinary surprise.
Château des Reynats, Ave. des Reynats, Chancelade–Périgueux;
33-5/53-03-53-59;
dinner for two $$$.

Château des Reynats.

The Dordogne River, seen from the town of Domme.

Lascaux II
The 17,000-year-old Cro-Magnon cave paintings at Grotte de Lascaux have been closed to the public since 1963. See replicas here instead.
Montignac-Lascaux;
33-5/53-35-50-10.

La Maison
Learn to cook Périgord classics with Danièle Mazet-Delpeuch. Two-day courses from $308, including one-night stay, all meals plus wine, and a visit to a truffle field.
Chavagnac;
33-5/53-51-00-24;
cooking-truffles.com

FIVE STOPS YOU SHOULDN'T MISS
In 1982, Charles Ceyrac, then mayor of Collonges-la-Rouge, formed *Les Plus Beaux Villages de France*, an organization dedicated to preserving France's most beautiful villages. Acceptance into the group isn't easy: besides good looks, a town must have architectural and historical interest—and fewer than 2,000 inhabitants. Of the 144 member towns, an impressive concentration lies in and around the Dordogne Valley. Driving the small country roads that connect them is an ideal way to see the best of the valley. Collonges-la-Rouge is perhaps the most spectacular of these; Monpazier, with the concentric rectangular layout that typifies the *bastide*, runs a close second. Here are five other favorites:

Domme
On a bluff high above the Dordogne River, this 13th-century *bastide* is notable for its views of the luminous green farmlands and surrounding villages, as well as for its unusual lamb chop–shaped town plan. Because of its central location, Domme fills up with tourists in summer, but in spring, when the simple houses are covered with purple wisteria, quiet prevails.

WHERE TO SHOP
In Sarlat, stores on the Place de la Liberté offer delectable foods such as foie gras and truffles. On Wednesdays and Saturdays, the outdoor market—one of the best in the Dordogne—fills the square.

Elie-Arnaud Denoix
Vin de noix (labeled apéritif de noix*) and plum* eau-de-vie, *in lovely gift bottles.*
Collonges-la-Rouge;
33-5/55-25-44-72.

Entre Cour et Jardin
Bright jacquard table linens; local pottery in earthy colors.
36 Rue St.-Jacques, Monpazier;
33-5/53-22-61-30;
couretjardin.com.

Moulin de la Tour
A 16th-century water mill with virgin walnut, hazelnut, and almond oils for sale. Tours available.
Ste.-Nathalène, Sarlat;
33-5/53-59-22-08.

WHAT TO DO
Musée National de Préhistoire
Cave paintings, Neanderthal skeletons, and tools in a 16th-century fortress.
Les Eyzies-de-Tayac;
33-5/53-06-45-45.

Grotte du Grand Roc
Guided walking tours of prehistoric caves deep in a hillside.
Les-Eyzies-de-Tayac;
33-5/53-06-92-70;
grandroc.com.

Extracting walnut oil at Moulin de la Tour, near Sarlat.

Geese at La Maison, Danièle Mazet-Delpeuch's farm and cooking school.

La Roque-Gageac

Seen from the banks of the Dordogne, tiny La Roque appears to emerge whole out of a rocky cliff. Ancient houses with *lauze* (stone slab) roofs climb straight up the bluff. Take the narrow path to the right of the stamp-size post office to the top of the town. There you'll find troglodyte caves—if you brave the rickety wooden staircases leading up to them.

Loubressac

Also designated an official *Village Fleuri* (flowering village), Loubressac is a hill town with walled gardens, exuberant pink hydrangeas, pretty ironwork lanterns, and fruit trees that bloom in springtime. In every direction, the village has breathtaking views of the green valley below.

Autoire

Ringed by rocky, verdant cliffs, Autoire is a cluster of striking medieval half-timbered houses with steeply pitched shingled roofs, several of which were built by nobility from nearby St.-Céré in the 15th and 16th centuries. A dramatic square clock tower dominates the sleepy, quintessentially Quercynois town.

Carennac

Larger and livelier than many of the other villages, Carennac borders the Dordogne and has its own babbling creek flowing through town. The larger manors have pointed towers and turrets, and gardens filled with pale apricot roses. A trail leads down to the river, and follows its tranquil bank. (Since Loubressac, Autoire, and Carennac are closely grouped in the eastern end of the valley, the three towns make a good circuit for a day trip.)

A half-timbered turret in Autoire.

A view over a bridge into Carennac, at the eastern end of the Dordogne Valley.

SEE ALSO
For more on the Dordogne:
New Wave Inns pp.94–95

Ma Vie en Rosé

AN AMERICAN HOTELIER AND AUTHOR LONGING FOR HER OWN VINTAGE FINDS PLENTY OF WINE WORTH BOTTLING AT A FAMILY-RUN VINEYARD IN THE PROVENÇAL TOWN OF PUYLOUBIER. BY JENNIFER RUBELL

PUYLOUBIER

Here was my fantasy: to create the perfect summer wine, something decent, light, and drinkable with anything, everything, or nothing.

I wanted it to be inexpensive enough to keep around by the case, refreshing enough to hit the spot on a hot summer day, and attractive enough to put on the table at lunches that go on until sundown. I wanted it for myself and for my friends. I wanted to serve it at parties for my book *Real Life Entertaining*,

which is all about doing things with plenty of style but no pretense or fuss. And in the end, I wanted it to be available to everyone else too. Since I'm already making it, I reasoned naïvely, I might as well sell it.

Gradually, my fantasy wine came into being. Through a friend, I found a producer whose wine making I could trust—his Châteauneuf-du-Pape Domaine du Vieux Lazaret is reliably excellent— and who was also willing to do a 200-case batch for

The vineyards at Domaine Houchart, in Puyloubier.

Photographs by Kevin Miyazaki

me; in the wine business, that's minuscule. I procured both an importer and a distributor. I sought—and gained—approval for the wine from the United States government, the French government, the state of New York (where I grew up), and the state of Florida (where my family's hotel, the Albion, and art museum are located). I hired a company in New York to design the label (brilliant designers, but no wine label experience), and slowly—it took many dozens of phone calls to various expediters, importers, and the winemaker himself—figured out all the necessary government-mandated wording. I discovered that printing wine labels to be used on a traditional bottling line is an art in itself, with plenty of its own rules: the grain must be horizontal; varnish is mandatory, for protection in shipping; self-adhesive and pressure-sensitive labels are newfangled no-no's. All the while, the winemaker was creating the actual wine in France.

Now here I am at Domaine Houchart, a 220-acre vineyard with a tasting room and winery located in the beautiful, tiny Provençal town of Puyloubier, population 1,671, walking through rows of vines with Jérôme Quiot, the man who has been making wine for me.

At first, Quiot appears to be a Provençal cliché: dark hair, slightly crooked teeth, handsome, and friendly, with the sort-of-but-not-quite-American energy of a French pop song. Look a little closer, though, and there's more to him than that. A fine red thread on the lapel of his cashmere jacket—the oh-so-subtle French symbol of knighthood in the Legion of Honor—is a clue that Quiot's world is larger than this vineyard. As a matter of fact,

*Bread and wine
at Houchart.*

his family is the largest landowner in Châteauneuf-du-Pape, 60 miles to the northwest. (As Quiot tells it, his ancestors helped start the French Revolution because with the aristocracy in place, they'd never have gotten the choicest parcels of land.)

But it was love—well, at least marriage—that brought Quiot to Puyloubier. His wife, Geneviève, née Houchart, was born and raised in these parts.

Her family members are laced through this community on either side of the Route de Cézanne. Her father made a pact with God to build a church in nearby Palette if the town was spared during World War II, and there stands the church, on Place Houchard (the mayor's office made a typo on the last letter). Madame Quiot's grandmother used to have Cézanne over for tea, but refused to buy his paintings, judging them to be of poor quality. Quiot's son was married in town to a woman whose childhood home is just down the road. To this man, in this place, all geography is either biography or *terroir*. His land tells stories, and his land makes wine. And, though his land makes many different kinds of wine, I'm here for the rosé.

Yes, my search for the perfect summer wine has led me to Provençal rosé, one with that typical floral- and berry-infused bouquet and a dry, high-acid finish. After years of being pooh-poohed as the wine cooler of wines, and unaided by the ubiquity of sweet, flat, cloying white Zinfandel, dry rosé is on the lists of serious restaurants, and seriously hip ones, across the country. Books have been written about it. And unlike the popularity of certain reds or whites, the chic of rosé (proof: Francis Coppola produces one named after daughter Sofia) isn't really about taste. It's about a warm-weather way of life that's easy, unpretentious, open, and ever-so-slightly tipsy. You don't delicately sip a rosé and discuss the notes of fruit and leather. You pour it, drink it, eat something, drink some more, and then

Cyclists passing through Puyloubier.

*To this vintner, in this place, all geography
is either biography or* terroir

*Puyloubier, in the foothills of
Mont Sainte-Victoire.*

147

you take an afternoon nap. You can even drink it with a couple of ice cubes—heresy with other wines, fine with rosé.

In the vineyard, Quiot picks up a handful of earth and slowly lets it drop—is there some secret instructional video for winemakers that teaches them all to do this?—revealing the rich, dark, fertile soil where the grapes for my newly bottled rosé were grown. We walk for about a half-hour, with Quiot talking passionately about everything he does to ensure that these vines are happy. We start heading toward the winery, but Quiot suddenly stops. "Here," he says, waving dramatically at a smallish plot of land picturesquely dotted with trees, a small hut, and heavily scented ground cover, "is my *petit bois*."

I ask Quiot why he would sacrifice usable land for a little area of found nature, expecting an explanation about sustainable agriculture and the need to maintain unplanted areas for the good of the vines. Instead, he draws me this picture: "In the summer, I come here with my son, a pizza, and a couple of bottles of rosé. That is why we keep it.

Sometimes we bring *saucisson*. Doesn't matter." Quiot and his son, Jean-Baptiste, sit together having lunch on an old bench surrounded by rosemary, thyme, and lavender, real-life *herbes de Provence*. I can imagine the wood-handled pocket-knife Quiot the elder uses to cut the *saucisson*. I smell all the herbs in full bloom. Yes, I'd keep a *petit bois* too, if it meant having picnics on the grass with my daughter every summer. I like that this man is making my wine.

We arrive at the winery, a concrete-floored room so simple, it makes you feel as if you could become a winemaker yourself. There are two presses for harvested grapes ("They cost $200,000 and we use them a few days a year, but what can you do?" Quiot asks, in that charmingly defeated French way); some stainless-steel tanks where the juice and skins are subsequently held—this 10-hour maceration is what makes rosé pink—and some larger sealed cement tanks; a cooling system; and a massive, cathedral-ceilinged storage room, where, incidentally, Quiot's son's wedding reception was held.

Lunch at Relais de Saint Ser, in Puyloubier.

Provençal lamb with tapenade at Relais de Saint Ser.

It's time to taste my wine. We mount a narrow metal staircase to a small yellow-walled tasting room with 360-degree views. After our 30-minute walk through the vineyard, the cool of the winery felt good, but up here the air is stifling. The room is filled with sunlight. Out the north window, there's the *petit bois*, and beyond that, Mont Sainte-Victoire, best known as Cézanne's favorite subject. To the west is Aix-en-Provence. To the east, just outside the window, are the vineyards of Domaine Houchart. In the room, there's just Quiot; Daniel Phillip Kim, a member of the Oxford Wine Circle's winning 1999 Varsity Wine-Tasting team (an '83 Margaux decided their fate in the final match against Cambridge); me; and a bottle of Real Life Rosé—my wine, my actual wine, not ready until now—sitting on the table surrounded by three glasses. The moment of truth.

Quiot pours a little wine into each of our glasses, and we hold them up to the Provençal light. Pink, but not too pink: perfect. We swirl the wine and put our noses in the glasses: strawberries, wildflowers, light cherries. Nice. Now, a sip each. Into the mouth, then a gurgle to aerate the wine. Quiot spits into the silver tasting spittoon; Daniel and I swallow. My first instinct is to take another sip. I'm overheated from our trek through the vineyard and the climb up to this aerie. I'm embarrassed to tell Quiot that this wine just simply hits the spot—no

Winemaker Jérôme Quiot and his son, Jean-Baptiste, enjoying a glass of rosé in the petit bois *(small wooded area) at Domaine Houchart.*

wine-tasting lingo comes to mind. Fortunately, Daniel pipes up: "Garden strawberries," he says, "And good acidity." I'm off the hook. But then Quiot looks at me, expectantly.

"It tastes like summer," I say, drinking some more.

And there it is. This is, in fact, the wine I'd wanted all along. It's fresh, bright, and easy to drink—especially on a hot day. It doesn't have the complexity of a great Bordeaux or Burgundy, but you don't want it to. It reveals itself quickly—berries, flowers, acidity, one, two, three—and then goes down easily. It is indeed a great wine for a picnic (Bring on the *saucisson*!) or a barbecue.

After the rosé tasting, we head to the nearby Relais de Saint Ser, a favorite lunch spot for local winemakers. At a few of the tables on the stone-walled terrace—including our own—people are passing around not-yet-labeled bottles of rosé they brought with them. After Quiot shakes a few hands, we sit down. A pile of croutons and some green-olive tapenade appear. The waitress brings us goat-cheese salads. I order the lamb chops. The food is simple, homemade. Mont Sainte-Victoire is behind us, and the view ahead, with Domaine Houchart in the distance to the left, is extraordinary. We drink my rosé. And it's perfect.

Travelers' Guide to Aix-en-Provence

WHEN TO GO

Provence is beautiful spring through fall. Harvest is mid-September to early October.

En-Vau, one of Les Calanques, on the coast near Cassis.

While in Aix...

Abbaye de Silvacane ❶
Aix-en-Provence ❷
Aubagne ❸
Bandol ❹
Barjols ❺
Brignoles ❻
Cassis ❼
Les Calanques ❽
Marseille ❾
Puyloubier ❿
St.-Maximin-la-Ste.- Baume ⓫
Sanary-sur-Mer ⓬
Toulon ⓭
Hyères ⓮

EXPLORING AROUND AIX

Puyloubier lies about 11 miles east of Aix-en-Provence, the former capital of Provence and Cézanne's spiritual home. Ancient and charming, Aix is also cosmopolitan and cool, with a large student population. Popular nearby coastal spots include the ports of Marseilles and Cassis, and the diving and fishing resort of Sanary-sur-Mer. A short car or boat trip away lie Les Calanques: deep, narrow inlets set between pine trees and white cliffs.

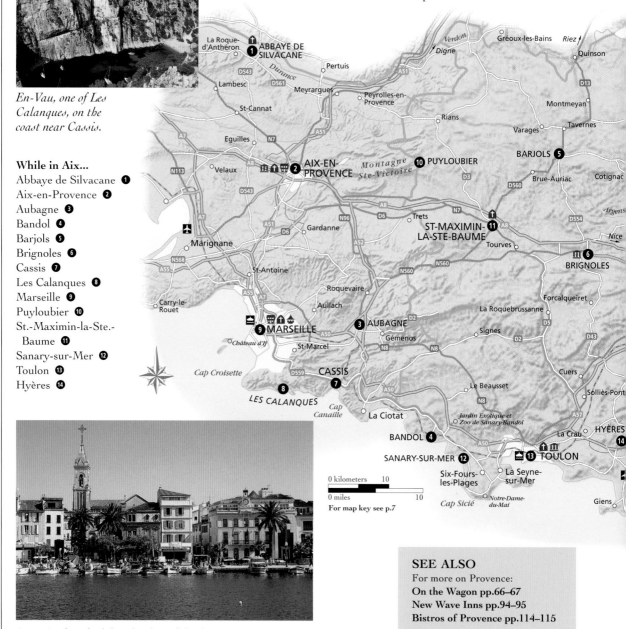

0 kilometers 10
0 miles 10
For map key see p.7

Boats in the colorful, palm-fringed harbor at Sanary-sur-Mer.

SEE ALSO

For more on Provence:
On the Wagon pp.66–67
New Wave Inns pp.94–95
Bistros of Provence pp.114–115

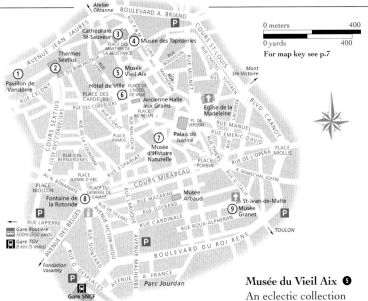

WHERE TO STAY

La Villa Gallici

Reservations are hard to come by at this 22-room Relais & Châteaux inn and garden oasis.

Ave. de la Violette, Aix-en-Provence; 800/735-2478 or 33-4/42-23-29-23; villagallici.com; doubles from $$.

WHERE TO EAT

Auberge du Relais de Saint Ser

13114 Rte. de St.-Antonin, Puyloubier; 33-4/42-66-37-26; dinner for two $$.

Le Clos de la Violette

Some of the finest cuisine in the south of France.

10 Ave. de la Violette, Aix-en-Provence; 33-4/42-23-30-71; closdelaviolette.com; dinner for two $$$$.

WHAT TO DO

Domaine Houchart

The vineyard grounds at Puyloubier are open to the public.

12 Rte. Départementale; 33-4/42-66-34-44; jeromequiot.com;

Houchart's main tasting room, an hour away in Châteauneuf-du-Pape, is open all year except Sundays.

5 Ave. Baron Leroy; 33-4/90-83-73-55;

WHAT TO READ

Two Towns in Provence By M.F.K. Fisher. Illustrates the food and daily life of Aix and Marseilles.

REAL LIFE ROSÉ

For information on where to buy the author's wine, Real Life Rosé, check out jenniferrubell.com.

TOP SIGHTS IN AIX

Cathédrale St.-Sauveur ❸

The 13th-century cathedral is noted for its walnut doors, Merovingian baptistry, and Romanesque cloisters. Its treasure is the Burning Bush triptych (1476) by Nicolas Froment.

Fontaine de la Rotonde ❽

This cast-iron fountain, built in 1860, is located at the western end of the Cours Mirabeau, Aix's finest street.

Hôtel de Ville ❻

This splendid building, built around a courtyard by Pierre Pavillon from 1665–70, stands in the center of a square now used as a flower market.

Musée des Tapisseries ❹

Apart from magnificent 17th- and 18th-century Beauvais tapestries, the museum has opera costumes and stage designs used in the annual Festival International d'Aix.

Musée Granet ❾

The city's main museum is in an impressive 17th-century former priory of the Knights of Malta. The collection includes archaeological finds and paintings by French, Italian, and Flemish artists.

Musée du Vieil Aix ❺

An eclectic collection of local memorabilia.

Muséum d'Histoire Naturelle ❼

Based in the Hôtel Boyer d'Eguilles, designed by Pierre Puget, and built in 1775, the museum has fine displays on mineralogy and paleontology.

Pavillon de Vendôme ❶

Constructed for Cardinal de Vendôme in 1667, this is one of Aix's grandest buildings. It houses Provençal furniture and works of art by Van Loo.

Thermes Sextius ❷

The town's mineral waters are used for a variety of spa treatments at this thermal bath.

Aix's 17th-century Hôtel de Ville.

151

Detail of a Chanel jacket at vintage shop Didier Ludot, in Paris.

PART FOUR
Arts and Culture

Living Rooms

PARIS

TOURING THE RECENTLY REENVISIONED, MASSIVE COLLECTIONS OF THE MUSÉE DES ARTS DÉCORATIFS AT THE LOUVRE REVEALS EIGHT CENTURIES OF FRENCH SAVOIR FAIRE. BY LESLIE CAMHI

I was gazing at the perfect pink town houses of Place des Vosges from a private balcony one summer evening as a fellow dinner guest, an auctioneer, spoke of the people who lived there as if they were his small-town neighbors. His family had owned the *hôtel particulier* next door for some three centuries, though he'd been the first to inhabit it. Former

ministers of culture, famous pianists, *femmes du monde*, and high-living art dealers—he had known them all and under his gavel, many of their goods had been dispersed. His conversation betrayed a very French passion for the souls of objects, an intuitive grasp of what the details of an interior might reveal about a person's private life. He let slip, for example, that he was installing three sinks

The Tuileries Gardens, seen from the museum's south side.

Photographs by Ditte Isager

in his master bathroom, leaving his domestic arrangements to my imagination. And he sighed with contentment over a purchase he had made at Drouot, the leading French auction house, that very morning—the bookcase of a turn-of-the-century pair, the desk of which had long been in his possession. He said it was like reuniting the scattered members of a single family.

I was in Paris to visit the Musée des Arts Décoratifs, which had recently reopened after a decade-long, $46 million renovation. A monument to the French *art de vivre*, housed in a 19th-century wing of the Louvre that has been restored to Beaux-Arts splendor, the museum's galleries and period rooms showcase eight centuries of Gallic taste in interior decoration.

It's a unique institution in France, in that its vast collection of some 150,000 objects—from medieval prie-dieus to Sèvres porcelain to an entire Art Deco Pullman car—was built almost exclusively from private donations. The 6,000 pieces on view when the museum reopened are spread out across 10 floors and arranged in roughly chronological order, punctuated by special displays, including a gallery devoted to the history of toy design and a room full of paintings by Jean Dubuffet donated by the artist in 1967.

So it is also home to a thousand ghosts. Some corseted lady, one imagines, spread her crinolines across the rich upholstery of that Second Empire sofa; some free spirit reclined on that tubular, 1920's lounge chair, dreaming of a Modernist utopia. The hands that trailed along that sinuous Art Nouveau

155

The bedroom of fashion designer Jeanne Lanvin, part of the reconstructed apartment at the Musée des Arts Décoratifs.

156

railing or raised a 17th-century glass to lips are never far from one's thoughts, as are the hands of countless, often anonymous artisans. In a country where the art of the past is considered part of the national patrimony, subject to regulations as strict as the appellation "Roquefort," such dependence upon private patronage is an aberration.

"It's linked to the origins of our institution, which was born in the 19th century out of the desire of individual industrialists and collectors," explained the museum's director, Béatrice Salmon. "At the time," she continued, "a museum of the decorative arts wasn't something the state considered indispensable." We were sitting in her office, one wall of which was covered with cartoon portraits of major benefactors that were slated to be installed along museum staircases. Furniture manufacturers and antiques dealers mingled with artists, collectors, and philanthropists.

In her airy top-floor study overlooking the elegant topiaries of the Tuileries Gardens, Hélène David-Weill, the institution's venerable yet sylphlike president, emphasized the intimate nature of each donation. "People gave the museum, for the most part, what they had lived with and loved," she said.

Every once in a while, the French rise up and burn their furniture. Not a single French throne survived the Revolution of 1789. Gustave Flaubert described the delirium of the hordes invading the Louvre's royal residences during the Revolution of 1848 as "redoubling to the continuous din of breaking porcelain and shards of crystal"; 23 years later, the insurgent mobs of the Paris Commune made bonfires of the royal curtains and canapés in the Tuileries.

Perhaps it was the memory of those earlier conflagrations, as much as the threat of industrial competition from London, that inspired a group of 19th-century businessmen to create a museum of the French decorative arts. Their aim was twofold: to elevate the standards of national production by setting examples of excellence before the eyes of their workers, and to educate the tastes of a public newly attuned to the consumption of luxury goods. An early version of the museum, installed at No. 3 Place des Vosges, was open late at night so that upholsterers, cabinetmakers, and seamstresses could visit it after their ateliers had closed. Later on, the state, rallying at last to the museum's cause, donated the Marsan Wing of the Louvre, its current location along the Rue de Rivoli, where it opened in 1905

(although within the precincts of the Louvre, the Musée des Arts Décoratifs is a separate institution).

Its focus on the "minor arts" of decoration also left it open to works that more traditional institutions, such as the Louvre, tended to shy away from. The museum was among the first in France to show African art and photography, and mounted key exhibitions of contemporary artists early in their careers, from Picasso to Daniel Buren. It still presides over two related museums, housed in the same wing of the Louvre and devoted to quintessentially French passions, fashion and advertising. (Farther afield, but also under its jurisdiction, lies the Musée Nissim de Camondo, a house that a Turkish-born Sephardic-Jewish banker, Moïse de Camondo, constructed on the eve of World War I, basing it upon the model of the Petit Trianon at Versailles and filling it with exquisite examples of Rococo furniture.)

Today, natural light floods through the oculi of a soaring central atrium (long obscured by successive

Cartoon portraits of donors along a museum staircase.

renovations), and the sweep of French history unfolds through things designed mostly for daily use. Galleries highlight specific techniques and styles, such as examples of the 18th-century mania for cabinets adorned with eye-popping geometric wood veneers, or the macabre *fin de siècle* penchant for decorative bats and dragons on everything from table legs and mirrors to wallpaper.

Despite the national focus, the museum's pieces show a history of constant exchange across borders, as Flemish, Chinese, and Italian influences (among others) have been absorbed and tempered by Gallic sensibilities. "Just look at European porcelain," Mme. David-Weill noted. "It began in Saxony, with manufacturers trying to surpass the achievements of the Chinese. So you can't say that it's a properly French tradition—it goes back even to the time of the Egyptians." Or consider a marvelously delicate writing table that once belonged to Madame de Pompadour, where the royal paramour may have sat writing love notes to King Louis XV. Its lacquered surface, inset with Orientalist scenes, imitates the Japanese, but in a blue that is classically French.

Because this is France, the history of desire is woven into these objects, and illicit passion has been among the greatest spurs to the creation and consumption of luxury goods. Witness the remarkable assortment of Lalique jewels worn by the expatriate American *salonière* Natalie Clifford Barney, all gifts (in a shade that matched the blue of her eyes) from her lovers: female poets and courtesans of the Belle Époque. There's also the fantastic collection of Boucheron tie pins—miniature boars' heads sculpted from sapphires, gold-and-enamel bees—offered to Nissim de Camondo (father of Moïse) by his mistress, a shady American divorcée from Baltimore.

On the fifth floor is a spectacular 19th-century bed cast in bronze—a throne, really, hung with velvet curtains and decorated with cupids and fleurs-de-lis—which another *grande horizontale*, Valtesse de la Bigne, left to the museum. She was among the models for Émile Zola's portrait of a prostitute, *Nana*; her legendary bed a tool of the trade with which she had made her fortune. Though royal heads may have rested upon its embroidered pillowcases, the Louvre would not have welcomed it. Here it's the centerpiece of a gallery devoted to the style of the great courtesans who were her contemporaries.

The veil that the French discreetly draw over their private lives is ever so slightly lifted in the museum's newly reconstructed period rooms, which conjure the ambience of different eras as they invite viewers into the intimate recesses of abodes. That sacred literary sanctuary, the cork-lined room where Marcel Proust composed *Remembrance of Things Past* in bed while tending to his allergies, is unfortunately not among them (it's at the nearby Musée de Carnavalet). But visitors can marvel at the luxurious bedchamber commissioned in the 1830's by the Baron William Hope, a Dutch-English banker so wealthy he lent money to King Louis-Philippe. Hope never married; did he repair to this room, with its brightly colored paneling, its walls covered in brilliant yellow-and-white silk damask, and its frieze of commedia dell'arte figures, alone or with one of his mistresses?

The changing whims of fashion are highlighted in the Cabinet des Fables, an elegant 18th-century boudoir intended for the wife of a wealthy tax collector in Paris (whose home was seized by the state in the wake of the French Revolution and whose rooms were transformed, a century later, into

A reconstruction of Baron William Hope's 1840 Louis-Philippe–style bedroom.

The nave of the museum, facing Rue de Rivoli.

the offices of a military governor). The paneling's pale-green and rose-colored moldings, which surround illustrations of scenes from La Fontaine's *Fables*—monkeys negotiating with foxes and the like—were covered in gold, and the entire ladylike confection rendered at once bolder and more vulgar. (Restorers have left evidence of both stages.)

Time stands still in the private apartments of couturier Jeanne Lanvin: a bedchamber, boudoir, and bathroom created between 1922 and 1925, with the designer Armand Albert Rateau, as a cloistered refuge where this consummate artist and businesswoman could retire in private or with intimate friends and relations. The silk wall coverings in her signature shade of blue have been reembroidered by Jean-François Lesage (son of the celebrated couture embroiderer); the perfect geometries of her bathroom, with its sculpted deer above a marble tub and its black-and-cream tiles, gleam once more. "These rooms were designed for a woman alone," said Hélène Guéné, the author of a recent book on the relationships in France between *haute couture* and interior decoration. "Everything turns around a very gentle and sophisticated idea of nature, like an enclosed garden behind whose walls one would speak of nothing but what interested her."

During the month of May 1968, as French students and workers joined in a general strike, and the paving stones of Paris served once again at the barricades, the Musée des Arts Décoratifs mounted an exhibition devoted to 20th-century chairs. No one at the time was thinking of sitting down, but the show remains a landmark in the history of design exhibitions. Today the museum's contemporary galleries reflect design's current internationalism as well as its reach, which has stretched into the houses of the masses.

"We've never been a museum of the art of the people," Béatrice Salmon said. "Our founders' insistence on French savoir faire and excellence from the nation's artisans always put us just alongside royal tastes. Of course, a peasant may have sculpted a wonderful pair of clogs. But the history of our institution and the reality of its collections lie elsewhere. Today, because of the industrialization and democratization of design, the same social categories aren't really valid anymore."

Designer trash cans for all! That was one cry never heard upon the barricades. But perhaps, in perusing these galleries, the revolutionary masses of the past might have found themselves reflected—or at least seen something they'd have liked to take home.

An extensive
collection of 20th-
century chairs.

Travelers' Guide to the Musée du Louvre

EXPLORING THE LOUVRE

The Musée du Louvre, one of the most important art collections in the world, dates back to medieval times. The original building—a fortress constructed in 1190 by King Philippe-Auguste to protect Paris against Viking raids—was replaced during the reign of François I by a Renaissance-style building. Over the following centuries a succession of French kings, emperors, and presidents enlarged and improved it. The latest addition is the collection of arts from Asia, Africa, Oceania, and the Americas in the Pavillon des Sessions.

The Musée des Arts Décoratifs, the Musée de la Mode et du Textile, and the Musée de la Publicité are housed in this wing.

The Jardin du Carrousel was the grand approach to the Tuileries Palace, which was set ablaze in 1871 by insurgents of the Paris Commune.

Cour Marly

Arc du Triomphe du Carrousel

The Carrousel du Louvre underground complex (1993), with galleries, shops, parking and an information desk, lies beneath the Arc du Triomphe du Carrousel.

The inverted glass pyramid brings light to the subterranean complex, echoing the museum's new main entrance in the Cour Napoléon.

Denon wing

The metal-and-glass pyramid designed by I.M. Pei (1989) is the museum's main entrance. It allows light down into the underground reception area.

Hall Napoléon is situated under the pyramid.

The Pont des Arts is a pedestrian bridge over the Seine that links the Cour Carrée of the Louvre with the Left Bank.

WHAT TO DO

Musée du Louvre
Rue de Rivoli, First Arr.;
33-1/40-20-50-50;
louvre.fr.

Musée des Arts Décoratifs
*(Also Musée de la Mode et du Textile and
the Musée de la Publicité.)*
107 Rue de Rivoli, First Arr.;
33-1/44-55-57-50;
lesartsdecoratifs.fr.

Pavillon
Richelieu

Cour
Puget

Cour
Khorsabad

Cour
Napoléon

Sully wing

The Salle des Caryatides
is named after the four
monumental statues
created by Jean Goujon
in 1550 to support the
upper gallery.

Cour
Carrée

The east façade has majestic
rows of columns by Claude
Perrault, who worked on
the Louvre with Louis Le
Vau in the mid-17th century.

The remains of the medieval moats dug
by Philippe-Auguste (12th century)
and Charles V (14th century) can be
seem in the excavated area.

*Architect I.M. Pei's pyramid cleverly
juxtaposes the new with the old.*

*The ornate Galerie d'Apollon has
three ceiling panels by Charles Le
Brun (begun in 1663) and a number
of large-scale stucco sculptures.*

SEE ALSO
For more on Paris:
Paris Modern pp.18–21
Puttin' on the Ritz pp.80–81
Coco Loco pp.190–191
For Versailles:
Biking Through Versailles pp.28–29

*Cliffside in Port-en-Bessin,
a view often painted by
Georges Seurat in the 1880's.*

Norman Conquests

NORMANDY

AN OLD PHOTOGRAPH LINKS AN AMERICAN COLLEGE IN WORLD WAR II WITH THE SUMMER RETREATS OF FRANCE'S INTELLIGENTSIA—AND THE HISTORY OF NORMANDY'S COASTLINE. BY CHRISTOPHER BENFEY

The late Victorians, our intellectual parents in so many ways, jettisoned the religious pilgrimage for a different kind of quest—the search for a landscape in key with their own inchoate yearnings. Paris and Rome retained their complicated allure, of course, but other places began to emerge from history's dustbin. For Marcel Proust and Claude Monet, Henry Adams and Henry James, a meander through Normandy was the intellectual pilgrimage at its multilayered finest. The austere stone architecture and poplar-studded pastures suggested a lost world of spiritual certainty and aesthetic decorum, a place where the secrets of the past opened up new meanings for the fraught and uncertain present. And so it was for me.

I would never have traveled to the Romanesque churches and channel beaches of Normandy had I not stumbled across an unassuming snapshot of Wallace Stevens among the photographs in the center of Peter Brazeau's biography of the poet. The black-and-white image, slightly blurred by bright sunlight, shows Stevens in his habitual business suit, seated on a lawn by a brick building next to a diminutive man with wavy hair and glasses. Brazeau's caption reads: "Jean Wahl and Wallace Stevens at Mount Holyoke College in August 1943, when Stevens lectured on 'The Figure of the Youth as Virile Poet.'" Now, I knew the lecture—a difficult meditation on the task of poetry to lift the spirit "in a

Photographs by Frédéric Lagrange

*Dives-sur-Mer, a small Norman
town, near Cabourg.*

leaden time"—and I knew the college, where I have taught for a number of years. The Beaux-Arts building in the background is Porter Hall, where I have my office. But who was Jean Wahl and what were these men doing on the lawn at Mount Holyoke on a summer afternoon in the middle of World War II? To find answers to those questions, I went first to the Mount Holyoke archives, then to various books, and, finally, to a 17th-century château in Cerisy-la-Salle, the heart of Normandy. What I learned, assembling the puzzle piece by piece, is that Mount Holyoke was a rich detour, caused by the pressures of war, in the complicated history of a series of exchanges among Europe's leading intellectuals, known as les *entretiens de Pontigny*—the Pontigny conversations.

Making art history at Mount Holyoke in 1943 (from left): André Masson, George Boaz, Lionello Venturi, and Marc Chagall.

Pontigny is a famous Cistercian abbey in the Burgundy region of France. There, beginning in the summer of 1910, a full-bearded humanist with medieval tastes named Paul Desjardins—imagine a French William Morris—would convene a group of writers, thinkers, and artists for 10-day informal conversations, or *décades*, on themes like "Man and Time" or "The Will to Evil" or "Is Civilization Mortal?" French writers dominated: André Gide and Paul Valéry were regular participants during the early years; later, the young Albert Camus and Jean-Paul Sartre gave the sessions a more political turn. But such Francophile Bloomsbury figures as Lytton Strachey, Dora Carrington, and Roger Fry came as well. Not many Americans were involved, though Edith Wharton stopped by one afternoon in her touring car and journalist Elizabeth Sergeant wrote that staying at Pontigny was like being at "a glorified, intellectual house-party."

If the conversation was sophisticated, the living arrangements were not. Strachey complained that the sanitary facilities at Pontigny were "crushing and inadequate," that his bedroom was literally a monk's cell. (He did enjoy flirting with Desjardins's son Blaise, whom he described as "largish, pale, [and] unhealthy," adding that he sang very well.) Gisèle Freund's photograph of philosopher Walter

Benjamin walking along the river by the abbey in the summer of 1938, twirling a flower between his fingers, has a particular poignancy—a moment of meditative calm about to be shattered. (In 1940, Benjamin was finally prevailed upon to leave Nazi-occupied France for Spain and eventual safe passage to America, but committed suicide in the border town of Port Bou.)

The Pontigny session in August 1939, co-sponsored by the London-based *Times Literary Supplement* in a gesture of Anglo-French solidarity, carried the ominous theme of "Destiny." It was interrupted by news of Hitler's invasion of Poland on September 1. A few months later the Nazis took over the old abbey, the Gestapo destroyed its archives, and that was the end of the *entretiens*—for the moment. They resumed three years later, beneath the elms and maples of the Mount Holyoke campus, in South Hadley, Massachusetts, for the duration of the war.

During the summers of 1942 through 1944, such European émigrés as the artist Marc Chagall and the philosopher Hannah Arendt met their American peers at what was named Pontigny-en-Amérique. When the exiles returned to France after the war,

Philosopher and poet Jean Wahl (at desk) heading a décade *in the summer of 1944 at Mount Holyoke College, where the colloquiums once held at Pontigny, France, continued during World War II.*

Jean Wahl (left) with Gustave Cohen of the École Libre des Hautes Études at the New School in New York and Helen Patch, chairwoman of Mount Holyoke's French department, on the lawn between talks, in 1943.

the *entretiens* returned as well, though not to Pontigny, which had by then passed into other hands. The international gatherings were held, and continue to be to this day, in the small Norman town of Cerisy-la-Salle, at the Desjardins family's other estate.

So it was to Cerisy that I traveled one summer for a special session, titled "De Pontigny à Cerisy," to be devoted to the nearly century-long history of Pontigny and its permutations, with a particular section on the years when the *entretiens* had been transferred to Mount Holyoke. There was also an accompanying exhibition in the Norman university town of Caen, with extraordinary photographs and documentation.

After a short drive from the cathedral town of Coutances, I arrived at the château at Cerisy-la-Salle, where professors and writers were just beginning to assemble in the quaint, heavy-beamed library to hear Professor Laurent Jeanpierre, a young scholar from the University of Paris, lay out his colorful account of the French invasion of Mount Holyoke, which he described as having been a far more "transatlantic and even global dialogue" than any held at Pontigny itself. He noted the importance for the history of modern art of a session held in the summer of 1944 that included the Abstract Expressionist Robert Motherwell, the Surrealist André Masson, and the young sculptor Louise Bourgeois. On that occasion, Motherwell delivered his first talk defending the claims of abstraction against the traditions of Surrealism. At that moment, Jeanpierre argued, one could see the first tremors of the seismic shift from Paris as the center of artistic innovation to New York, and of the new wave in modern painting. Another session brought together the anthropologist Claude Lévi-Strauss and the linguist Roman Jakobson, founders of what came to be known as Structuralism, a theory of language and culture that revolutionized the study of literature. Jeanpierre was arguing that France and the United States had been allies not just in a military sense, but intellectually as well. At the time, and even now perhaps, this was something that seemed at once heartening and impossibly remote.

Pontigny-en-Amérique (or "Pont'holyoke," as it was affectionately called) was the brainchild of an enterprising Mount Holyoke professor named Helen Patch. She wanted to create an advanced summer school for French language and culture, drawing on the expertise of the many French artists and intellectuals living in exile in New York. The exiles, in turn, wondered whether there might be a way to resume those spirited conversations at Pontigny that had been interrupted by the war—and whose themes suddenly seemed more urgent than ever. Patch suggested to her old Sorbonne mentor, the medievalist Gustave Cohen, who was living in New York and teaching at the New School, that Mount Holyoke, the oldest women's college in the United States, could serve as a reasonable facsimile of Desjardins's monastery at Pontigny. And Cohen knew just the person to organize such a thing: Jean Wahl, the man next to Wallace Stevens in the faded photograph.

Born into a Jewish family in Marseilles, Wahl was uniquely positioned, by temperament and training, for the role of cultural intermediary between France and America. His father was a teacher of English, and Wahl grew up fully bilingual, as at home with *Huckleberry Finn* as with *The Count of Monte Cristo*. He was a philosopher and a poet whose first major book, published in 1920, was a study of American pragmatist philosophy that introduced the ideas of William James to a French audience. (An early existentialist, he had created a stir when he failed Jean-Paul Sartre in a graduate course.) Wahl was precisely the kind of "cosmopolitan Jew" the Nazis reviled. The Gestapo arrested him immediately following the occupation of Paris and subjected him to weeks of interrogation and torture; during lulls in the horrific routine Wahl read *Moby Dick*, in English, and wrote short poems. (The Germans, noted Wahl's friend Henry Church, "were told to mistreat him and being obedient did so.") Wahl was incarcerated at the concentration camp of Drancy, where, with thousands of other

The cathedral, as seen from the castle, in Caen.

French Jews, he awaited the death trains to Auschwitz. In a 1945 *New Yorker* profile, Wahl described his unlikely escape in the back of a butcher's truck, hiding among the carcasses. Emaciated and scarred, he made his way to Marseilles, where he boarded one of the last refugee ships to the United States. He arrived in New York on August 1, 1942, and was quickly drawn into the planning group for Pontigny-en-Amérique.

Wahl had a double vision for the Mount Holyoke *décades*. They were intended to be, first of all, acts of intellectual resistance, the cultural counterpart of de Gaulle's Free French in London. But Wahl also wanted them to serve as occasions for French-American dialogue, sealing culturally an alliance crucial to the eventual liberation of France. So, as the Allies prepared to reclaim Europe from the Nazis, Jean Wahl marshaled his intellectual troops

Training for the Deauville races on the tidal flats of Cabourg.

*The American cemetery at Omaha Beach,
honoring those who died there on D-Day.*

in Massachusetts. Wahl's outdoor discussions, which
were accompanied by the sounds of jets flying
overhead from the nearby Westover Air Reserve
Base and of Navy Waves training on campus, were
intense. Poet Marianne Moore wrote of her
admiration for Wahl, the "elfin and most touching
exile." "An unselfish experiment like that of the
Pontigny Committee," she added, "leaves a certain
memory of exaltation, and a great desire to be of
service to those who have suffered, and fought so
well." Word spread of this remarkable occasion.
Time sent a reporter, who learned that Mount
Holyoke students thought Wahl was "cute." The
Times Literary Supplement announced that the "spirit
of the Abbey" had found a "sanctuary" in the United
States. Proceedings were published in the
prestigious *Sewanee Review*.

The OSS (forerunner of the CIA) dispatched an
agent to Mount Holyoke to see what the fuss was all
about. What the agent found, on the whole, was a
gathering of tolerant, humanistic, and nonsectarian
intellectuals and artists. When the mathematician
Jacques Hadamard was asked whether, after a
French victory, ethnic Germans should be evicted
from France, he responded forcefully in the
negative. The French, in that case, Hadamard said,
would be mimicking the crimes of the Nazis.

Sitting in the library of the château at Cerisy,
listening to Professor Jeanpierre and the ensuing
conversation, I began to feel the special mood
of these occasions that had spanned a century
and crisscrossed the Atlantic. Jacques Derrida,
the eminent philosopher and godfather of
deconstruction, flew in later that night from Nice
and described Pontigny-Cerisy as a "counter-
institution" outside the normal routines and rituals
of academic life. "One never knows truly, totally,
what, in the future, is going to happen when one
comes to Cerisy," Derrida remarked.

For me, such reflections drove home the
transatlantic events of the summer of 1944. As the
students left the Mount Holyoke campus to make
way for debates on such questions as the fate of
20th-century art, Eisenhower was making his
decision to invade Normandy. Omaha Beach is just
an hour's drive from Cerisy, past stone villages and
dairy farms. The landscape—perhaps because my
mind kept shifting between Cerisy and South
Hadley—reminded me of New England. But Henry
Adams, a passionate Normandy pilgrim, had also

noted the resemblance, believing the inhabitants of
these granite coasts to be "as hard and practical a
fact as the granite itself." My own vague image of
the American Cemetery, drawn from films and
history books, hardly prepared me for the sheer
emotional impact of Omaha Beach. The sky was
ashen and the surf down the cliffs was rough and
roiling. A single row of pines lined the bluffs
overlooking the landing beaches. Spreading out on
the level turf as far as the eye could see was an ocean
of white crosses, some 10,000 of them, like doves
alighted on the grass. Each cross, with an occasional
Star of David mixed in, gave four stark pieces of
information: the soldier's name, rank and regiment,
home state, and date of death. The afternoon I visited,
it was rare to hear an American voice, though I heard
Italian, Japanese, German, and French spoken—
reverently, and in hushed tones. The graves were a
painful reminder that American soldiers would again
be risking their lives far from home.

A few minutes eastward, the no-frills fishing
village of Port-en-Bessin, which served as a

communications center for the Allies, offered another perspective on the invasion. Port-en-Bessin is the main port with access to the city of Bayeux, and its docks were lined with brightly colored fishing boats. On the high ridge above the town, a steep five-minute hike from the docks, the German gun emplacements looked like medieval redoubts, with vivid, blood-red poppies sprinkled among the stones. On the way down, I came upon a bronze easel with a marker explaining that the Pointillist Georges Seurat, along with his disciple Paul Signac, had come often in the 1880's to paint this view. I found myself thinking that not only was this landscape layered with historical memory—from William the Conqueror to the D-day landings—but that every traveler has brought his or her own fresh interpretation to the scene, stitching the present to the remote past.

Here and there along the coast, you can still see signs of how, in the 19th century, fops and dandies from England and France turned the austere Norman coast into the most popular seaside resort in Europe. In the sleepy resort town of Cabourg, a few miles east of Port-en-Bessin, which Proust immortalized as Balbec in *Remembrance of Things Past*, the casino where the young novelist whiled away the time is still standing. The Proust family were themselves close friends of Desjardins, the founder of Pontigny, who described Proust in 1888 as a "Persian prince" with "huge gazelle eyes and languorous eyelids…a collector of pleasures." Though Cabourg has not missed the opportunity to capitalize on its association with Proust—the boardwalk is named Promenade Marcel-Proust—it is possible even here to see Normandy as the author first saw it.

When the beaches—miles of dunes and oyster bays—ceased to amuse, the cathedrals were waiting. At the turn of the 20th century, such cultural pilgrims as Proust, Monet, and Henry Adams turned Normandy into a different kind of vacation spot, one where the traveler could idle—while his motorcar and driver waited—in the landscapes and mindscapes of the medieval past. "The architectural highway," as Adams wrote in his great travelogue *Mont-Saint-Michel and Chartres*, "lies through Coutances, Bayeux, Caen, Rouen, and Mantes." Elstir, Proust's fictitious painter, who is in part modeled on Monet, is enraptured by the carved bas-reliefs in the little church at Balbec (Cabourg). "What exquisite trouvailles came to the old carver,"

Proust wrote, "what profound thoughts, what delicious poetry!"

Monet himself had studied the great cathedral façade in Rouen, which Henry James had described as "magnificently battered, heavy, impressive." Monet, by contrast, tried to give the massive cathedral an airy, polychromatic lightness. Though he painted canvas after canvas—30 in all—he had a recurring nightmare about the cathedral: "It fell on me [and] seemed to be pink or blue or yellow."

I was having a little daydream of my own, tracing in my imagination my progress across Normandy from steeple to steeple across the hill towns and battlefields. Proust had remarked that you see French country towns long before you get to them, their stone spires shifting with your changing perspective. Something similar had happened with my own quest for Pontigny-en-Amérique. I found a pocket of American history in the heart of Normandy and of French history in western Massachusetts. From her rooms at Mount Holyoke, Marianne Moore had experienced the same sense of being in two places at once. As she wrote to Elizabeth Bishop in the summer of 1943: "You should see the tiny hemlock cones at Holyoke; and hear the bells, which clang sonorously every hour and half hour so you feel as if you were in Europe."

The Memorial Chapel at the American cemetery, at Omaha Beach.

On the high ridge above the town, a steep five-minute hike from the docks, the German gun emplacements looked like medieval redoubts, with vivid, blood-red poppies sprinkled among the stones

The town of Port-en-Bessin.

Travelers' Guide to Normandy

GETTING THERE

From Charles de Gaulle Airport in Paris you can get a connecting flight to Rouen, Caen, or Le Havre, or you can rent a car for the trip north (it's just 97 miles to Rouen, 158 to Caen). Trains run between the major Norman cities, but you'll need a car to see the region in depth.

EXPLORING NORMANDY

Normandy's rich historical sights and diverse landscape make it ideal for touring by car or bicycle. Rewarding coastal drives and good beaches can be found along the windswept Côte d'Albâtre, and the Cotentin Peninsula. Further south is one of France's most celebrated sights, Mont St.-Michel. Inland, follow the meanders of the Seine Valley, passing cider orchards and half-timbered houses along the way, to visit historic Rouen and Monet's garden at Giverny.

Rugged cliffs on the Cotentin Peninsula.

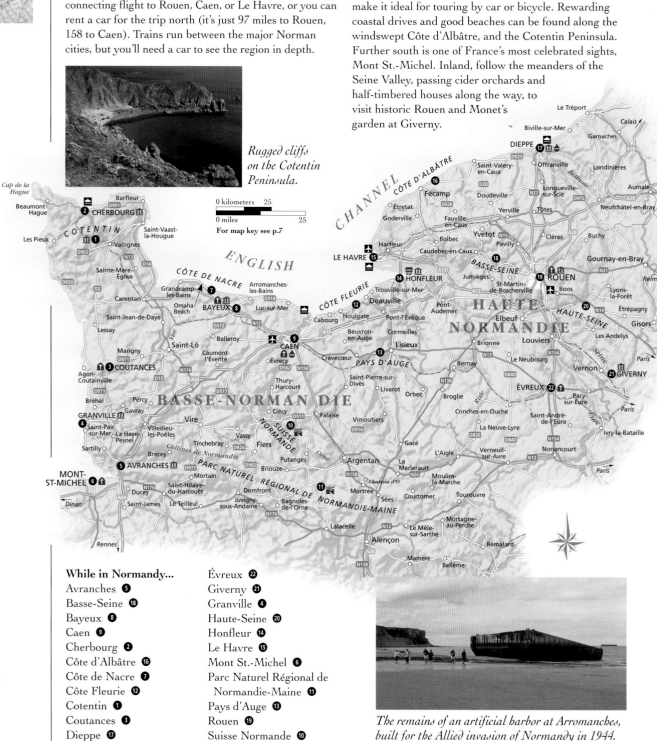

0 kilometers 25

0 miles 25

For map key see p.7

The remains of an artificial harbor at Arromanches, built for the Allied invasion of Normandy in 1944.

The Grand Hôtel, in Cabourg.

WHERE TO STAY

Château La Chenevière
An 18th-century manor house with walled rose gardens and 30 acres of parkland, a few minutes' drive from the coast.
Escures-Commes, Port-en-Bessin;
33-2/31-51-25-25;
lacheneviere.fr;
doubles from $$$.

Grand Hôtel de Cabourg
Proust stayed in room 414 of this Belle Époque building. Rooms on the north side face the sea.
Promenade Marcel-Proust, Cabourg;
33-2/31-91-01-79;
mercure.com;
doubles from $$$.

Hôtel Château d'Agneaux
A 13th-century castle, now a 12-room inn and restaurant, in the Vire Valley of central Normandy, a half-hour's drive south from Omaha Beach.
Ave. Ste.-Marie, St.-Lô, Agneaux;
33-2/33-57-65-88;
chateau-agneaux.com;
doubles from $$.

WHERE TO EAT

Gill
Chef-owner Gilles Tournadre scours local markets daily to assemble rich regional dishes such as squab with foie gras ravioli.
8–9 Quai de la Bourse, Rouen;
33-2/35-71-16-14;
dinner for two $$$.

Café de la Digue
Order a plate of Normandy oysters and bulots (whelks) at this beachfront café, next door to the Grand Hôtel.
Promenade Marcel-Proust, Cabourg;
33-2/31-91-62-48;
lunch for two $$.

WHAT TO DO

Cerisy-la-Salle
Just outside Coutances, on the road to Bayeux, this 17th-century château is where the colloquiums that began at Pontigny are held from the end of May to the start of October. Open to the public on Thursdays in July and August; available for group tours in summer with prior reservations.
33-2/33-46-91-66;
ccic-cerisy.asso.fr

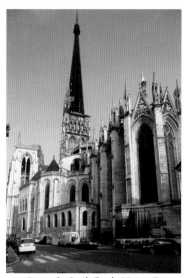

Rouen's Cathédrale Notre-Dame.

Église St.-Étienne
One of the greatest of the early Romanesque churches, in the Abbaye aux Hommes monastery complex.
Place Monseigneur des Hameaux, Caen;
33-2/31-30-42-81.

Le Mémorial de Caen
This World War II–focused peace museum commemorates the leadup to D-Day, the event itself, and the historical significance of the battle. The museum also organizes five-hour guided tours of the D-day landing beaches.
Esplanade Eisenhower, Caen;
33-2/31-06-06-44;
memorial-caen.fr;
tours from $76.

Above the sea, Mont St.-Michel is one of the most enchanting sights in France.

Sacré Bleu

. . . AND GREEN AND YELLOW AND RED, TOO. SINCE THE 1930's, ARTISTS HAVE TURNED A HAND TO THE WINDOWS OF FRANCE'S OLDEST CHURCHES, AND THE RESULTS COULDN'T BE MORE HEAVENLY. BY MIRIAM ROSEN

Some of the best 20th-century art in France can be found in its churches. And not only in Vence, at the chapel Matisse decorated for the Dominican nuns, or in Ronchamp, where Le Corbusier built the whimsical Notre-Dame-du-Haut in reinforced concrete. You also find it in cathedrals, abbeys, and parish churches that date from the Middle Ages to the 19th century. Fitted out with state-of-the-art stained glass, such churches have become sacred galleries, where contemporary figurative and abstract painting—even sculptures—are on display.

The idea has provenance. As early as 1937, a dozen modern painters were invited to design the windows at Notre Dame de Toute Grâce du Plateau d'Assy in Haute-Savoie. The project, a source of some controversy anyway (many of the artists were neither particularly pious nor particularly interested in depicting religious scenes), was interrupted by the outbreak of World War II. After the war, however, the extensive damage to many French churches, coupled with the rise of a postwar abstraction, lent new momentum to the attempt to revive *"l'art sacré."* Its driving force, Father Couturier, put it this way in a letter to Le Corbusier: "To set off this renaissance, this resurrection, it is safer to turn to geniuses without faith than believers without talent."

The first completed non-figurative project was by Alfred Manessier, an up-and-coming painter of the School of Paris, who created seven windows for the 18th-century country church of Les Bréseux, beginning in 1948. Though a modest venture, it was followed by, among others, Jacques Villon's windows (1956–7) and then Marc Chagall's (1958–68) in Metz, which depict the Passion of Christ; Maria Helena Vieira da Silva's abstract glass panes in Reims (1967–76); and Joan Miró's Surrealist scenes in the medieval cathedral of Notre Dame at Senlis

(1977). From that time sacred spaces continued, on scales both large and small. In the vast cathedral of Nevers, such distinguished and diverse contemporary painters as Gottfried Honegger, François Rouan, Claude Viallat, and Jean-Michel Alberola have each designed groups of windows.

Since the late 1980s, this dialogue between present-day aesthetics and religious faith has taken a slight turn: no longer merely paintings transferred to glass, specially commissioned windows are now produced through an intense collaboration between artists and a new kind of master glazier, armed with innovative techniques. In a number of respects, what many still regard as a breakthrough in the manufacture of glass came in 1975, when a 36-year-old self-taught artist named Jean-Pierre Raynaud was invited to create 64 windows for the former abbey of Noirlac, which had been founded in the 12th

Église St.-Sulpice de Varennes-Jarcy, a 13th-century church just outside Paris.

Photographs by Jean Marie del Moral

Robert Morris's hallucinatory window "waves" in St.-Pierre de Maguelone, in the marshes near Montpellier.

The windows in these churches are no longer merely paintings transferred to glass but the product of intense collaboration between contemporary artists and master glaziers

century by monks of the rigorous Cistercian order. He assembled 160,000 panes of unornamented glass to achieve a stunning integration of the spare vocabulary of the past with the resolutely contemporary syntax of 1970's Minimalism. Neither figures nor colors were permitted in Cistercian churches, and the sole designs on the windows were formed by the leading. As for the artist, his major work until then was a house he had built for himself entirely out of white ceramic tiles. Raynaud's asymmetrical grid patterns create almost imperceptible gradations of transparency that not only illuminate the interior but, as the light changes, suggest the passage of time—from one hour, one season, one century, to the next. This same relationship to light and space has been variously pursued in Conques, Digne, Lognes, Villeneuve-lès-Maguelone, and Varennes-Jarcy.

In Conques, painter Pierre Soulages devoted years of research to developing glass with the right translucency, producing a series of window screens that resemble alabaster for the venerable pilgrimage church of Ste. Foy. The most striking aspect of Soulages's work is its understatement. Viewed from the outside, the glass strips take on the bluish cast of the natural light they reflect, complementing the surrounding sandstone and echoing the blue slate roof, while inside, the glass assumes the warmer tones of the unreflected light.

At Villeneuve-lès-Maguelone in 2002, artist Robert Morris drew his inspiration from the architecture of the fortress-like former cathedral of St.-Pierre de Maguelone and from its singular location—a tiny spit of an island in the marshes that line the Mediterranean coast near Montpellier. Here the undulating forms of the glass windows are meant to

An interior view of a Robert Morris window at the 11th-century St.-Pierre de Maguelone.

A master glazier at the Ateliers Duchemin, in Paris, innovators in the art of glass-making.   179

Carole Benzaken's tulip motif in Égli[...]
St.-Sulpice de Varennes-Jarc[...]

French artist Christophe Cuzin's stained-glass windows for the 19th-century village church at Lognes, near Paris.

evoke waves, which seem to move with the ebbs and flows of light.

New York–based sculptor David Rabinowitch designed the windows and the liturgical furniture as well—pews, lecterns, pulpits—for the starkly Romanesque Cathédrale Notre-Dame-du-Bourg, in Digne. Inside, shimmering crystal disks of mauve, blue, yellow, and green emerge as if from a primal void. The parishioners are as enthusiastic about the effect as the artist, whose visual language both captures the religious character of the space and suggests a more universal spirituality.

Though achieved by strikingly different means, the same quality is evident in St.-Martin, the late-19th-century parish church in Lognes, a village outside Paris. French painter Christophe Cuzin, known for conceptual work that blurs the line between what lies inside and what lies outside the canvas, redefined the church's interior with swaths of color. "Everything in the building was false," he explains. "It was a tiny country church modeled on a cathedral. What's true

is color, because it's only light. It's something mystical."

To achieve the effect he sought, Cuzin painted the walls blue, red, and green, and the windows, created in collaboration with the Ateliers Duchemin, one of France's most innovative glass-making studios, were similarly minimalist: barely tinted panes of industrial glass that illuminate the walls so that they seem to glow from within. Similarly, too, the jewel tones of Carole Benzaken's tulip motif, an allusion to the Stem of Jesse, the tribe from which King David descended, saturate the plain stone walls of the Église St.-Sulpice de Varennes-Jarcy, near Paris, in a play of color and shadow.

The fusion of these contemporary works with their historic settings is striking. Yet you never get the feeling that you are looking at "a Soulages" or "a Morris," much less walking through an exhibition. The best way to appreciate the windows is simply to sit down and watch the light change, perhaps the closest many of us will come to transcendence.

181

Travelers' Guide to Contemporary Stained Glass

STAINED GLASS IN FRANCE

The renaissance in French stained glass inspired by Father Alain Couturier gained momentum in the period after World War II, with the urgent need to restore and rebuild churches—and their windows—that had been damaged by bombing. In the post-war years, a new generation of stained-glass artists began to emerge, with their own ways of interpreting this traditional art form.

0 km   100
0 miles   100
For map key see p.7

Calais · Dunkerque
Boulogne · Lille · Douai
Abbeville · Arras · Amiens
Dieppe
Cherbourg · Le Havre · Rouen
Caen · **8** SENLIS · REIMS **3** · Verdun · Thionville **1**
St- Malo · PARIS · **6** LOGNES · METZ
Brest · Argentan · Chartres · **12** VARENNES-JARCY · Strasbourg
Rennes · Orléans · RONCHAMP **9**
Lorient · **14** GIEN · **10** LES BRÉSEUX
St- Nazaire · Tours · Vierzon · NEVERS · Dijon
Nantes · Saumur · Bourges · **2**
Cholet · BRUÈRE-ALLICHAMPS **15**
La Rochelle · **13** PLATEAU D'ASSY
Limoges · Lyon
Clermont-Ferrand · Vienne
Arcachon · Valence
5 CONQUES
7 DIGNE
Menton
Montpellier · VENCE **4** · Monaco · Nice
Biarritz · Toulouse · Marseille · Cannes
11 · Toulon
VILLENEUVE-LÈS-MAGUELONE
Perpignan

Stained-glass gazetteer...

Bruère-Allichamps **15**
Conques **5**
Digne **7**
Gien **14**
Les Bréseux **10**

Lognes **6**
Metz **1**
Nevers **2**
Plateau d'Assy **13**
Reims **3**
Ronchamp **9**

Senlis **8**
Varennes-Jarcy **12**
Vence **4**
Villeneuve-lès-Maguelone **11**

A Marc Chagall window at Notre-Dame de Reims.

The Chapelle du Saint-Marie du Rosaire, in Vence, which was decorated by Henri Matisse.

VISITING CHURCHES

Check with the local tourist office if you plan to go to a church or chapel, as it may be open only a few hours each day.

Abbaye de Noirlac
Windows by self-taught artist Jeanne-Pierre Raynaud; guided tours available.
Bruère-Allichamps.

Cathédrale de St.-Cyr
Contemporary windows by Gottfried Honegger, François Rouan, Claude Viallat, and Jean-Michel Alberola.
Nevers.

Cathédrale Notre Dame
This Gothic cathedral in the heart of a medieval town features surrealistic scenes by Joan Miró.
Senlis.

Cathédrale Notre-Dame-du-Bourg
Stained glass and liturgical furniture by David Rabinowitch, an American sculptor.
Digne.

Cathédrale St.-Étienne
Gothic cathedral containing windows by Jacques Villon and Marc Chagall.
Metz.

A distinctive disk-shaped window by Christophe Cuzin at St.-Martin, in Lognes.

Cathédrale St.-Pierre de Maguelone
Windows by Robert Morris, an American sculptor.
Villeneuve-lès-Maguelone

Chapelle du Saint-Marie du Rosaire
Vibrant windows and a whitewashed chapel designed by Matisse.
Vence.

Église Ste.-Foy
Windows by Tachiste painter Pierre Soulages.
Conques.
(See pp. 36 and 43.)

Église Ste.-Jeanne d'Arc
The interior of this church in the Loire Valley glows with stained glass by French artist and designer Max Ingrand.
Gien.

Église St.-Jacques
Portuguese artist Maria Héléna Vieira da Silva created abstract glass panes for the north and south transepts.
Reims.

Église St.-Martin-de-Lognes
French painter Christophe Cuzin's colored glass disks.
Lognes.

Église St.-Sulpice
French painter Carole Benzaken's tulip-motif windows. Guided tours available.
Varennes-Jarcy.

Notre-Dame de Reims
The windows in the last chapel to the rear of this cathedral were designed in 1974 by Marc Chagall.
Reims.

Notre Dame de Toute Grâce du Plateau d'Assy
A mountain church with stained glass by Marc Chagall, Georges Rouault, Henri Matisse, Fernand Léger, Alfred Manessier, Jean Bazaine, and others.
Plateau d'Assy, Haute-Savoie.

Notre-Dame-du-Haut
Le Corbusier's Modernist church, with his windows to match as well.
Ronchamp.

Ste.-Agathe des Bréseux
Abstract designs by Alfred Manessier can be seen in this 18th-century church.
Les Bréseux.

Carole Benzaken's window at Église St.-Sulpice de Varennes-Jarcy.

Detail of Max Ingrand's stained glass at Ste.-Jeanne d'Arc, in Gien.

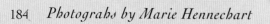

184   *Photograbs by Marie Hennechart*

Coco Loco

VISITING CHANEL'S LEGENDARY HAUNTS IN PARIS—FROM THE RITZ HOTEL TO THE PALAIS ROYAL—IS A CAPTIVATING WAY TO GET TO KNOW THE FASHION ICON HERSELF. BY LYNN YAEGER

PARIS

There is a famous story about the time fashion designer Paul Poiret stopped Gabrielle "Coco" Chanel on the street in Paris and gazed disdainfully at her shockingly simple frock, an early version of what would become her iconic little black dress. "Who are you in mourning for, mademoiselle?" sneered the man who put women in cascades of Belle Époque velvet. She witheringly replied, "For you, monsieur."

Maybe it's because she was such a tough cookie. Or that she managed to look as chic in 1970 as she did in 1910. Or that she rose from the humblest peasant domicile to the poshest Parisian salon. Not to mention that, with her brass-buttoned suits, jaunty costume jewelry, and comfortable spectator pumps, she almost single-handedly invented modern dressing. Whatever the reason, for years I've been unreasonably fascinated by Chanel and with her Paris, the city of her dreams, the place where she vanquished the ghosts of her impoverished girlhood and scaled the heights of artistic triumph. One spring, after years of trips to Paris but never a good opportunity to indulge in some sustained Chanel hunting—looking up her old haunts and seeking out early examples of her clothing and jewelry designs at the city's best markets and vintage boutiques—I finally managed to set a few days aside.

Ideally, any Chanel-centric trip includes a stay at the Paris Ritz, where Coco lived for the better part of her life. In her honor, I repair to the Bar Vendôme, ensconcing myself on a little velvet chair and checking out the lapdogs, which are frequently better dressed than their owners. (Even Chanel, champion of casual attire, might wince at the

outfits on some guests in her old residence.) The maître d' frowns subtly at a jeans-and-sneakers–clad guest, but softens when he spots the giant Birkin bag on her arm. I wonder if he's impressed with the Chanel ballet slippers I am wearing: a perfect combination of practicality and style, modernity and elegance, and comfortable enough for endless walks around Paris in search of Coco's footprints.

I convince a concierge to let me take a peek at the $9,700-a-night Chanel suite, a vast two-bedroom space with a spectacular view of the Vendôme column. Pricey as the suite is, the concierge tells me, it's always solidly booked during the fashion collections. (He doesn't mention one of the less savory aspects of Chanel's life story: she lived here as a result of an affair with a German officer during the war. Never at a loss for words, when she was arrested for collaboration she was rumored to have said, "Really, sir, a woman of my age who has the chance of a lover cannot be expected to look at his passport.") The suite is indeed lavish, and the Ritz has managed to incorporate many of Chanel's favorite things: a coromandel-inspired armoire hides the television; there's a blackamoor doorstop; sheaves of wheat are arranged near the massive fireplace. I half expect Sergei Diaghilev or Jean Cocteau to pop in looking for Mademoiselle.

It's a short walk from the Ritz to the gardens of the Palais Royal, where I can imagine the small and determined designer, bundled in tweed, heading to see her friendly enemy Colette, who had a flat on the square for many years. (Colette once described Chanel as "a little black bull.") I'm meeting with Didier Ludot, owner of what is perhaps Paris's most eminent vintage shop, which is tucked into the arcades of the Palais Royal. At the moment, Ludot doesn't have an iconic little black dress in the house, but he does have an equally hard-to-find little black coat from the twenties, with silk flowers appliquéd to its cuffs. Chanel is generally credited with introducing the revolutionary look of that decade: the dropped waist; the slouchy silhouettes; the radical minimalism that made it easy for shopgirls to resemble duchesses (and vice versa). I want this coat desperately, but so does Ludot. "This I'm not

A sea of C's in the Paris Chanel boutique, at 31 Rue Cambon.

185

An antique Chanel dress at
Didier Ludot, a vintage shop
in the Palais Royal.

Pastries at Angelina, Coco Chanel's favorite teahouse.

selling!" he laughs. Nor is he parting with a pale chiffon dress from the 1960's, the identical one that Romy Schneider—Chanel considered her the ideal woman—once wore. "Karl wants to buy it! But I say no!" Ludot says gleefully, referring to Karl Lagerfeld, who took over the House of Chanel in 1983.

A few blocks from Ludot's shop is Angelina, the historic Rue de Rivoli tearoom that Chanel was known to frequent, taking rare breaks from her notoriously nonstop workdays. The room is far more Poiret than Chanel, with its riot of elaborate crystal chandeliers, ivory-and-gold–painted *boiserie*, and pastoral murals. Next to me, a woman in a knitted suit, slender as a reed, digs with abandon into a giant cream puff. Most likely she doesn't know it, but she owes quite a debt to Chanel. No, it's not the joy of dessert (Coco favored plain food, and not much of it). It's that slinky suit, the living embodiment of Chanel's much-quoted maxim that "fashion does not exist unless it goes down into the streets. The fashion that remains in the salons has no more significance than a costume ball."

A working woman who scraped her way out of a charity orphanage in rural Saumur, Coco Chanel arrived in Paris in 1909 (on the arm of a wealthy gentleman), determined to take the town by storm. She began as a milliner, decorating little straw boaters with buckles and ribbons—quite a

The designer at work in her studio in 1954.

departure from the massive hats adorned with dead birds that fashionable women of the time balanced on their heads. Her simple chapeaux were admired by the beau monde, who saw her wearing her own creations and demanded to know who had made them. Chanel convinced her rich boyfriend to set her up in business; he agreed, thinking it was just a lark. He was wrong.

By 1920, Chanel had added clothing to her repertoire, and like her hats, her outfits were unlike anything Paris had ever seen. She wore sweaters borrowed from her male friends at a time when such nonchalant cross-dressing was practically illegal; she employed jersey, formerly used only for fishermen's shirts, for her little black dresses. Somehow these disparate elements—the tweedy overcoats; the frocks based on Biarritz bathing suits—looked just right in post–World War I Paris.

Chanel purchased an 18th-century building on a narrow street across from the back entrance of the Ritz and opened her first couture salon. She kept an apartment over the store as a place to house her own clothes and host dinner parties. Here, at 31 Rue Cambon, the business is still based. The address is so renowned that letters addressed simply Chanel, Paris are promptly delivered; it's rather like Santa Claus, North Pole, I think.

As it happens, my friend Bernice Kwok-Gabel, the former senior press officer for the Metropolitan Museum of Art's Costume Institute, is also in town.

Miraculously, having worked with Chanel executives on the Met's 2005 blockbuster Chanel exhibition, Bernice is able to wangle a tour for me of Chanel's apartment, which isn't open to the public. It is as pristine as a gallery installation, and I'm agog at seeing in person so many iconic items that I have previously glimpsed only in photographs: her coromandel screens, her blackamoors, her Jacques Lipchitz sculptures, the sheaves of wheat she kept strewn by the fireplace, the divan she reclined on in a photograph by Horst. Chanel would arrive at 31 Rue Cambon every morning via the Ritz's back door; the hotel's porter would call ahead so the staff could spray the building's staircase with her celebrated perfume, No. 5. As I descend from her apartment, I linger for just a minute on the fifth step (the designer had a mysterious, lifelong affinity for the number five), where Chanel would perch and view her fashion shows in the mirror. The aroma of No. 5 is just discernible in the air.

The next morning, I set off for the St.-Ouen antiques market, where fiery-haired Olwen Forest

Vintage jewelry at Olwen Forest's stand, at St.-Ouen.

has a stand and displays what may be the best collection of vintage Chanel jewelry in the world. "I'm a nutcase about these things," she tells me, then goes on to explain why so many wealthy collectors are obsessed with Chanel's fake baubles. "They have all the real gold they could ever want, and anyway, costume can be rarer than fine jewelry." She reaches into a showcase to show me examples of Coco's legendary accessory designs: Maltese crosses made of bottle green glass; haute couture pearls, half gray and half white; an Art Nouveau–inspired Indian pendant. A pair of earrings shaped like miniature perfume bottles catches my eye. It turns out they're from the eighties and were created by Lagerfeld; Forest and I agree that some of his work is as witty as Chanel's.

It's a lovely afternoon, and I decide to stroll down Rue Gabriel in search of the apartment where Chanel lived when she first arrived in Paris. Alas, the address no longer exists, but I find something even better: Scarlett, a fancy vintage store located off nearby Avenue Montaigne, a street as chic in Chanel's time as it is today. Scarlett has a trove of those not-very-old artfully raveled Chanel jackets, along with a lot of other relatively affordable pieces. A camellia necklace with a dropped pearl is around $900; a classic black quilted-leather handbag with the trademark chain is available for a hundred more and shares space with many, many double C–embellished purses.

It may be an unwitting testament to the paradox of Coco Chanel's own life that Galeries Lafayette offers designer collections right next to more prosaic garments. I dip into the vast department store on the Boulevard Haussmann (truth be told, I always find an excuse to visit when I'm in town). On the hyperbusy main floor, within the Chanel boutique, my journey comes full circle. About 100 years ago, Chanel purchased the straw boaters she needed for her hat business in this very store—so new was she to the trade that she didn't know about buying wholesale. Now, in this cream-and-black bower, a rendering of Mademoiselle's distinctive, sharp profile dangles from a costume bar pin and decorates the toe caps of Chanel's famous two-toned ballet slippers. They are almost exactly like the ones I'm wearing.

A video display inside the Chanel boutique.

A Chanel-era
métro station.

Travelers' Guide to Designer Paris

WHERE TO STAY

Paris Ritz
15 Place Vendôme;
33-1/43-16-30-30;
ritzparis.com;
doubles from Ⓢ Ⓢ Ⓢ Ⓢ.

WHERE TO EAT

Angelina
226 Rue de Rivoli;
33-1/42-60-82-00;
tea for two Ⓢ Ⓢ.

Detail of a tweed tailleur.

WHERE TO SHOP

Chanel
The fashion house's original store.
31 Rue Cambon;
33-1/42-86-28-00;
chanel.com.

Didier Ludot
20 Galerie Montpensier;
33-1/42-96-06-56;
didierludot.com.

Galeries Lafayette
40 Blvd. Haussmann;
33-1/42-82-34-56;
galerieslafayette.com.

Olwen Forest
Stands 5 and 7, Allée 3,
Marché Serpette,
110 Rue des Rosiers,
St.-Ouen;
33-1/40-11-96-38.

Scarlett
10 Rue Clement-Marot;
33-1/56-89-03-00.

AVENUE MONTAIGNE

One of Paris's most fashionable
streets is the Avenue Montaigne, off
the Champs Élysées in the Eighth
Arrondissement. Here's where to shop.

Boutique Prada ❺
*Signature bags, shoes, and leather goods
are displayed on the ground floor, while the
clothing is upstairs.*
10 Ave. Montaigne;
33-1/53-23-99-40.

Chanel ❷
*Classic pieces such as braided tweed
jackets and two-toned shoes—as well as
Lagerfeld's more daring designs—are
displayed in this branch.*
42 Ave. Montaigne;
33-1/40-70-12-33.

Christian Dior ❶
*The gray-and-white decor is a chic
backdrop for the wide range of items,
from lingerie to evening wear.*
30 Ave. Montaigne;
30-1/40-73-54-44.

Emanuel Ungaro ❹
*This shop carries the less expensive U
line, plus Ungaro's main collection.*
2 Ave. Montaigne;
33-1/47-20-28-82.

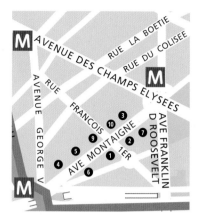

Jil Sander ❼
*Minimal and modern, just like the clothes.
Sander's trouser suits, cashmere dresses,
and overcoats are displayed on four floors.*
56 Ave. Montaigne;
33-1/44-95-06-70

Joseph ❻
*The largest of the four Joseph stores in
Paris, selling knitwear, evening wear,
and accessories*
14 Ave. Montaigne;
33-1/47-20-39-55

Max Mara ❿
*The Italian women's wear label is known
for its well-cut jackets and suits. The
trendier Sportmax line is also sold here.*
31 Ave. Montaigne;
33-1/47-20-60-79.

Nina Ricci Mode ❸
*After treating yourself to the gorgeous
lingerie or jewelry, go around the corner
to the Ricci Club, on Rue François, where
the menswear collection is sold.*
39 Ave. Montaigne;
33-1/40-88-64-42.

Valentino ❾
*Sophisticated clothes for the society set
and casual looks for the younger shopper
are displayed in this marble boutique.*
17–19 Ave. Montaigne;
33-1/42-66-95-94.

A Chanel window display.

190

"In order to be irreplaceable, one must always be different."
—Coco Chanel

The Chanel suite at the Paris Ritz.

SEE ALSO
For more on Paris:
Paris Modern pp.18–21
Puttin' on the Ritz pp.80–81
Living Rooms pp.162–163

191

Contributors

Christopher Benfey *is a professor of American literature at Mount Holyoke College. He has written for the* New Republic *and the* New York Review of Books. *His most recent book is* The Great Wave: Gilded Age Misfits, Japanese Eccentrics, and the Opening of Old Japan *(Random House).*

Kate Betts *is an editor-at-large at* Time *and an editor at* Time Style & Design. *She has written for* Vogue, Glamour, *the* New York Times, Food & Wine, *and* Time.

Leslie Brenner *is editor of the* Los Angeles Times Food *section and author of six books, including the novel* Greetings from the Golden State *(Henry Holt).*

Joan Juliet Buck *is a critic and novelist, and former editor-in-chief of* Paris Vogue.

Leslie Camhi, *a New York–based cultural critic, writes about the arts for the* New York Times, *the* Village Voice, Vogue, *and numerous other publications.*

Linda Dannenberg *has written nine books on France, including* New French Country *(Clarkson*

Potter). She has written for Town & Country, *the* Los Angeles Times, *and the* Wine Spectator.

Matt Lee *and* **Ted Lee** *are Travel + Leisure contributing editors and authors of* The Lee Brothers Southern Cookbook: Stories and Recipes for Southerners and Would-be Southerners *(W.W. Norton).*

Christopher Petkanas *is a special correspondent for* Travel + Leisure.

Frank Rose, *a contributing editor for* Wired, *writes extensively about the media and the entertainment business. His work has also appeared in* Esquire, Fortune, *and numerous other publications.*

Miriam Rosen *is an art critic based in Paris.*

Jennifer Rubell, *a contributing food editor for* Domino, *is the author of* Real Life Entertaining *(HarperCollins).*

Lynn Yaeger *is a contributing editor for* Travel + Leisure, *and a staff writer for the* Village Voice. *She also writes for* Vogue *and the* Atlantic Monthly.

Publisher's Acknowledgments

Dorling Kindersley would like to thank Casper Morris, Iorwerth Watkins, and John Plumer for their help and advice on the maps in this book, Romaine Werblow in the DK Picture Library for sourcing images, David McDonald for DTP work, and Karen Morgan for design assistance.

Original design by Stuart Jackman.

Picture Credits

The publisher would like to thank the following for their kind permission to reproduce their photographs:

Picture Key: a = above; b = below; c = center; l = left; r = right; rh = running head; t = top; f = far

1 Christopher Baker; **2–3** Andrea Fazzari; **4** Kevin Miyazaki; **5**bl Andrea Fazzari; **5**tr Joanna Van Mulder; **5**br Marie Hennechart; **6–7** Fernando Bengoechea; **10–17** (except rh) Martin Morrell; **20**bl Martin Morrell; **22–27** (except rh) Benoît Peverelli; **29**tr L'Etablissement Public du Musée et du Domaine National de Versailles; **30–41** (except rh) Christopher Baker; **42**br Christopher Baker; **44–53** (except rh) Fernando Bengoechea; **56–57** & **58–103**rh Andrea Fazzari; **58–65** (except rh) Benoît Peverelli; **68–79** Andrea Fazzari; **82–94** (except rh) Matthew Hranek; **96–101** (except rh) Marie Hennechart; **103**t & b Marie Hennechart; **104–105** & **106–151**rh Joanna Van Mulder; **106–113** (except rh) Guy Bouchet; **114**tl Guy Bouchet; **115**tl & tr Guy Bouchet; **116–125** (except rh) Andrea Fazzari; **128**t & b Andrea Fazzari; **130–139** (except rh) Lisa Linder; **141**b Lisa Linder; **142**bl & br Lisa Linder; **144–149** (except rh) Kevin Miyazaki; **151**bl Kevin Miyazaki; **152–153** & **154–191**rh Marie Hennechart; **154–161** (except rh) Ditte Isager; **164–173** (except rh) Frédéric Lagrange; **175**tl Frédéric Lagrange; **176–181** (except rh) Jean Marie del Morel; **183**tc & br Jean Marie del Morel; **184–186** Marie Hennechart; **187**t Marie Hennechart; **187**b Henry Clarkson/Condé Nast Archive/Corbis; **188**t & b Marie Hennechart; **189** Getty images; **190**cl Marie Hennechart; **191** Marie Hennechart.

All other images © Dorling Kindersley. For further information see **www.dkimages.com**